Railways
Revived

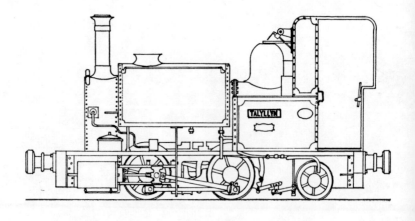

Railways Revived

An account of preserved
steam railways

P. J. G. Ransom

Faber & Faber

First published in 1973
by Faber and Faber Limited
3 Queen Square London WC1
Printed in Great Britain by
Butler & Tanner Ltd Frome

ISBN 0 571 09972 6

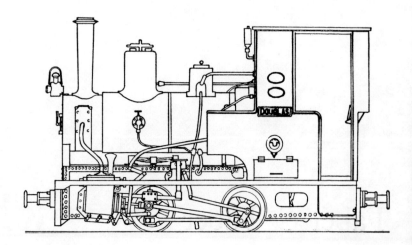

Contents

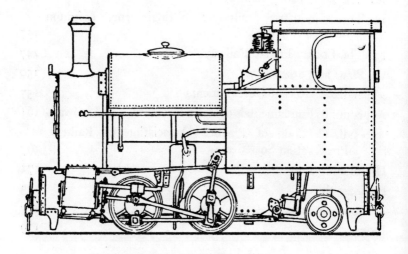

Plates

Maps

Graph

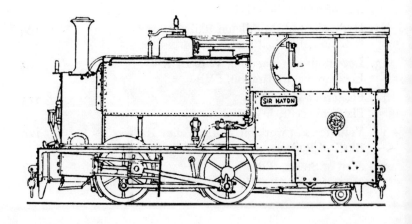

Foreword

'From little acorns, mighty oaks do grow.' In this book Mr. Ransom describes all the railway branches of the oak, some already sturdy limbs, others of more recent growth but all helping to make up a tree of most impressive stature. When we planted the Talyllyn Railway acorn 22 years ago, we never dreamed it would grow into anything like this.

The pioneers of any flourishing new movement are usually regarded with almost superstitious awe as though they were soothsayers, possessing an almost uncanny gift for forecasting the future. So let me say at once that in 1951 we had grave doubts about the future of our own project and that if we had been told that it was destined to be only the first of many similarly successful ventures we would have been frankly incredulous.

There were several reasons for such scepticism. In the first place, we grossly underestimated the extent of the support in money and manpower which the railway preservation movement would attract. So much so that when the Festiniog Railway project got off the ground in 1954 it caused some misgivings at Towyn, our fear being that there would not be a sufficient number of enthusiasts to support even two similar projects.

Again, in 1951 it seemed only yesterday that British Railways had announced their new standard range of steam locomotives and there seemed no reason to foresee that the steam locomotive was so soon to become obsolete. The Beeching axe had not yet fallen, closures had been comparatively few and Britain's railway system was still reasonably complete. Running narrow-gauge railways alone seemed to fall within the practicable scope of amateurs, and if anyone had told us that within the next twenty years volunteers would be successfully running a number of standard-gauge branch lines we would have said that he needed his head examining.

These two then unforeseen factors, the rapid disappearance

from commercial service of the steam locomotive and the virtual elimination of the branch line, swiftly transformed the whole railway preservation scene in a way that was quite unpredictable. 'Man is in love and loves what vanishes', as the poet Yeats once so truly wrote. From a battalion, railway preservationists have become an army, while the public flocks to see steam locomotives at work and to revive nostalgic memories of bygone journeys by branch line steam trains.

This book is a descriptive catalogue of preserved railways in Britain. It deals with the history of each railway both before and after rescue and gives an excellent factual summary of its present state. Mr. Ransom has achieved much more than this, however. He skilfully captures the particular character and atmosphere of each preserved line. In this distinctive character they are akin to the old British railway companies of pre-grouping days. As it was then, so it is now; such individuality is the outward manifestation of the pride, the loyalty and the creative aspiration of those who work for them. In an age of uniformity such diversity is as refreshing as it is essential to our well-being.

L. T. C. Rolt

I

Steam trains and volunteers: why and how railways are preserved

'I had no idea such a strange sub-world existed,' remarked the new step-sister-in-law to my wife. They were meeting for the first time to discover that both were married to men whose obsession was to disappear in the direction of the nearest steam engine. Not just to look, but to do something: polish it, shovel coal into it, pull trains with it.

This book is a sort of entry to that strange sub-world—or, rather, to a part of it. It deals only with the British Isles and only with railways which have been 'preserved'—that is, they have been rescued from being closed or dismantled and have subsequently revived. In many instances rescue took the form of a voluntary preservation society. All railways described are run wholly or partly by volunteers. All, too, use steam locomotives. Their loco-motives, though 'preserved', are not static, like those in museums, nor restricted, like those in railway preservation depots. They pull scheduled trains which carry passengers or freight from one place to another according to time-table.

As preserved—or revived—railways continually develop, I describe them as I found them in 1971. Developments since then are described in Appendix A. Despite my opening quotation, running such railways has grown from being rather an esoteric pursuit into a popular hobby, and many of the railways themselves have become tourist attractions of great importance.

I hope this book will interest tourist passengers who would like to know what makes these railways tick; and also those people who, while deeply involved in running any one of them, would like to know what makes the *others* tick.

There is much variety in preserved railways. The first to be established were in North Wales, but such lines are now to be found in localities from Devon to Fife, and Sussex to the Isle of Man. Their surroundings include not only wild mountains but peaceful countrysides and grimy industrial towns. This variety is matched in other aspects: locomotives range from over a century old to almost new, and from the smallest shunting engines to the largest express locomotives. Gauge of track—the width between the rails—ranges from standard 4 ft. 8½ in. down to as narrow as 1 ft. 3 in. And there are as many different ways of running a preserved railway as there are preserved railways.

I describe 14 railways in detail, showing how they originated, how they are run, and indicating the extents of train services and the types of locomotives to be found. For those who want precise details of train times or locomotive stocks, there are many annual publications.

What are these railways for? Why *are* railways preserved and revived?

There are really three reasons. Elements of each are found on each railway, though one is usually predominant. Which it is varies from line to line. There have also been many specific reasons, technical and historical, which have stimulated preservation and reopening of particular railways.

Of the general reasons, the first is to perpetuate and preserve the past in the form of steam trains, a means of transport now virtually extinct in Britain. But from the 1840s, when the basis of a national railway network had been established, until the 1920s, when the internal combustion engine had been developed far enough for road competition to become serious, railways had almost a monopoly of inland transport over distances of more than a few miles. Travel by puffing steam train was familiar to everyone —as familiar as travel by car or bus is now. Since the late 1920s, many railways have been closed, as a result of road competition, and on those that survive diesel or electric power has, with very few exceptions, replaced steam. So this reason is compounded of education, sentiment and idealism.

The second reason is to provide enjoyable recreation for volunteers who run and maintain preserved railways. With this is linked a satisfying way of life for any permanent and temporary staff, who are often, in effect, full-time paid volunteers. It is remarkable that as soon as a means of transport becomes obsolete people, who are often not conscious of its history, perpetuate it for its own sake.

MAP 1

Locations of Railways
Described

Dundee
LOCHTY

Edinburgh

Scotland

Isle
of
Man
IOMVSR

R&E

NORTH
YORK
MOORS

EMBSAY
Leeds
WORTH
VALLEY
MIDDLETON
Bradford

Liverpool

o Manchester

FESTINIOG
Stoke o
FOXFIELD

NORTH
NORFOLK

W&L
TALYLLYN
CHASEWATER
o Wolverhampton
Birmingham

SEVERN
VALLEY

Wales

England

LBNG

London

S&K
R.H.&D

BLUEBELL

Brighton

DART VALLEY
o Torquay

Both riding on horses and sailing in boats, for instance, are obsolete in Britain as transport, yet extremely popular as recreation. The point is relevant to the next paragraph also.

The third reason is to provide attractive entertainment for visitors, tourists and holiday-makers who ride in the trains. Some of them do not appreciate the previous two reasons, and may consider a steam train a sort of outsize fairground ride; but the greatest

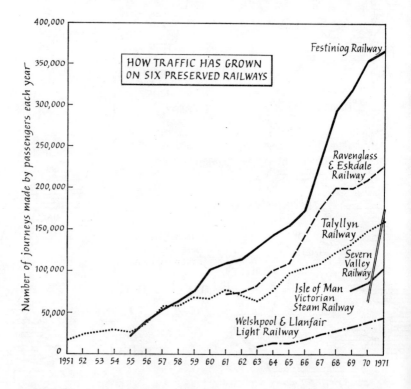

part of preserved railways' income is derived from them and a great deal of effort goes into meeting their needs. In this, preserved railways have much in common with zoos: popular places to take the children for a day out, but with, nevertheless, a more serious purpose behind them. Where zoos are concerned with conservation and indeed the survival of rare animals, preserved railways are concerned with survival of steam trains.

There is a further reason noticeable on some preserved railways. Despite high hopes by their promoters it is usually in practice so insignificant (Middleton Railway excepted) that I regret to say I almost forgot to include it. It is to provide a public transport service. With holiday-makers and day visitors, however, preserved steam railways enjoy great and increasing popularity. The graph on page 14 shows the numbers of journeys made by passengers on some of the principal lines since 1951 when the first, the Talyllyn, was established.

The Wales Tourist Board has produced a sort of league table showing the 50 most popular tourist attractions in Wales in 1970, in terms of numbers of visitors. The Festiniog Railway comes third, Talyllyn Railway 13th and the Welshpool and Llanfair Light Railway 31st. Other railways shown in the table are the Snowdon Mountain Railway at 12th place, the Vale of Rheidol Railway 14th and the Fairbourne Railway 21st. And this is in Wales, which is more dependent on tourism revenue, relative to population, than any other country save only Austria and Switzerland.

I have, I hope, many readers who do not consider themselves experts in the technicalities of steam railways. They may wish to read appendix B, a description of steam railway fundamentals, before continuing, for such knowledge is necessary to understand what follows.

Even I, who have been a voluntary railwayman for nearly 20 years, find it difficult to realize that, on one railway or another, every task involved is tackled by volunteers, with the exception of the heaviest overhauls to locomotives. It is difficult to appreciate when visiting the Worth Valley Railway, for instance, that all those officials in impressive railway uniforms, all those men in overalls, massive spanner in grimy hand, who look out from under engines to watch the train go past, and all the other people working on the railway, are volunteers. They all have full-time jobs else-where to earn their livings, and are present on the railway in their spare time or on holiday, just like the passengers.

People working on a railway fall into two categories: those who run the train service and those who maintain the railway and its equipment. For the first, the clock is master, and reliability and forethought are vital attributes. Only with the forethought born of experience are staff—booking clerks, driver, fireman, guard, signalmen, controller—in the right place at the right time doing the right task to ensure that a train runs according to the time-table; only with forethought are supplies of everything from coal to coffee available when needed. To such people satisfaction comes, at the end of the day, from knowledge of a job well done.

In the second category, people are not dominated by the clock so much, though they may be by the calendar. For instance, sufficient locomotives must be in running order for peak holiday traffic. Mechanical aptitude is essential and satisfaction comes from creative work as rolling stock is overhauled and track relaid.

In either category, however, team-work on a grand scale is needed—yet people who like railways enough to work for them voluntarily are often nothing if not individuals. Perhaps the most important attribute of all is tolerance of the idiosyncrasies of others.

Volunteer railwaymen come from every walk of life; indeed one of the most rewarding by-products of being one is meeting such people. There is a sprinkling of the House of Lords, and the House of Commons too. There are people whose professional expertise is valuable in running a preserved railway: they include 'real' railwaymen, mechanical and civil engineers, fitters, engineering apprentices, telecommunications experts, builders, accountants, lawyers and company directors. There are all the others whose professions are more or less irrelevant but who become, with time and training, expert in whatever railway department they choose. Backgrounds known to me include, in no particular order, civil servant, manager, salesman, clerk, draughtsman, printer, journalist, scientist, clergyman, doctor, dentist, photographer, airline officer, housewife, schoolmaster, student and retired person. I have heard of a freelance double bass player, and I was delighted to meet recently a volunteer locomotive fireman who really was, in working hours, a fireman: the sort that puts fires out!

Somewhere in the administrative set-up of most preserved railways, and often the first thing to be formed when one is projected, is a society, association or club. These, according to legal jargon, are 'unincorporated bodies' (which sounds rather horrible!) Cost of forming them is low and formalities are few; they should have a committee, a constitution and a set of audited accounts presented to members once a year. To be eligible for full membership of the Association of Railway Preservation Societies, which is described shortly, they need these and much else besides. Often societies, once established, sponsor groups or branches of members in various localities.

One of the snags to an unincorporated body is that all its members may in some circumstances be equally liable for all its debts and liabilities. These include debts for work done or materials supplied, and damages for negligence. Running a railway offers plenty of scope for such things to arise.

Members' liability is minimized when a preserved railway is operated by a limited liability company. Links between society and company vary from line to line, but whatever the circumstances there are various forms of company which recur. These are companies limited by guarantee, and companies limited by shares; and, old-fashioned but still occasionally met with, railway companies established by Acts of Parliament, mostly in the nineteenth century, to build and run railways.

At this stage the author wishes to make it clear that he has no pretence of being an expert in company law! The first need of anybody setting out to preserve a railway is a good lawyer.

A company is an incorporated group of persons considered as a legal entity, with liabilities, powers and property distinct from those of its members. In a company limited by guarantee, the form generally adopted by groups which do not intend to distribute a profit, liability of members is limited to the amount they guarantee to pay if the company is wound up. Often this is equivalent to one year's subscription.

Obtaining a railway is sometimes an expensive business, and one of the ways to raise the cash is to sell shares in a company which is to acquire and run it. This necessitates a company limited by shares. Liability of its members is limited to the amount, if any, which the company has not called up on shares which members have agreed to purchase. Usually, share companies are formed where it is intended to distribute a profit; railway preservationists, however, are idealistic and some of their share companies do not intend to do so. The legal adviser to the A.R.P.S. suggests a hybrid company would be useful—with shares for those who put up the money and also limited by guarantee for those who wish to be members but are unable or unwilling to commit capital.

A 'private company' may neither have more than 50 members nor invite the public to subscribe for shares. A 'public company' may do both but is governed by strict rules.

Sometimes unincorporated societies, being loose-knit, elect trustees as legal custodians of their property. A trust comes into existence when one or more persons hold property on behalf of others. One special type of trust is a charity: its beneficiaries are usually the general public. Under present law charities enjoy tax advantages, notably that they may recover income tax paid by members who covenant subscriptions to them. Groups preserving railways appear to be on the borderline of qualifying as charities, depending on their constitutions and aims. In 1971 the only preserved railway operated by a charity was the Middleton Railway.

In some small preserved railways, subscription-paying members belong to the body which operates the railway. These railways are Welshpool and Llanfair, Middleton, Sittingbourne and Kemsley, Leighton Buzzard and Foxfield. Other railways have a two-tier structure. In some instances, an operating company is controlled by a preservation society, as on the Talyllyn, Bluebell and Worth Valley railways. Otherwise the railway is operated by a company and there is a separate supporting organization; formal links between the two range from very close to non-existent.

Organizations which preserve and revive railways come together themselves in various associations. The most important is the Association of Railway Preservation Societies. Its aims are to further mutual co-operation of such societies, promote publicity on their behalf and encourage high standards. Full membership is not granted lightly. Applicants must conform to a strict code of practice. This strengthens the association in dealings with the British Railways Board and official bodies, and gives the public a yardstick by which to judge the soundness of any preservation scheme. I include the code in full as appendix C.

There are lower grades of membership: associate and private. The advantage of these is to give promoters of new preservation schemes access to the association's advice and experience while schemes are still in their formative stages. Over the past few years, as branch lines were closed and steam locomotives withdrawn, railway preservation schemes multiplied. Some were viable, some were not, some duplicated one another. The association has achieved order out of confusion—not by dictation but by negotiation and persuasion. Its task continues.

The A.R.P.S. caters for societies preserving railway equipment as well as those involved in operating preserved railways. Often possessions of the former—locomotives, carriages—are housed and run on the railways of the latter. With two-tier preserved railways it is usually the society rather than the operating company which belongs to the association. Almost all the railways described in this book have a connection with it. Meetings of the A.R.P.S. are held on members' railways and provide an opportunity for representatives to see behind other members' scenes and exchange news and gossip!—as well as conducting business.

The operating companies have their own trade association in the Association of Minor Railways, which works closely with the A.R.P.S. It is a 1970 revival of an association of the same name which was established in 1938 but last met in 1952. Membership is open to any railway operating a scheduled public service and so includes many purely commercial lines.

The Welsh lines also belong to the Narrow Gauge Railways of Wales Joint Marketing Panel. Its slogan is *Great Little Trains of Wales*. Publicity material and posters are produced jointly with the Wales Tourist Board and each member railway distributes the time-tables of all members in its own locality.

Standard-gauge railway preservationists get together at the Standard Gauge Convention in October. The 1971 event was an intensive 10.0 a.m. to 10.0 p.m. affair with sessions on finance and housing (for preserved railways and equipment), much discussion and a talk by railway artist David Shepherd.

Where does the money come from? Sources of funds for railway preservation societies are members' subscriptions, donations by members and well-wishers, draws and loans, with or without interest. Railway revenue is derived from fares, car parks, catering, sale of souvenirs and books, and provision of facilities for film companies. Industry is most helpful in providing goods and services 'on the cheap'.

Another source of revenue for several preserved railways is operation of a railway letter service. Letters are carried by the trains and bear stamps issued by the railway in addition to ordinary postage stamps. The original purpose of railway letters, when introduced in the 1890s, was quicker delivery than normal post; today, their attraction to preserved railways is principally that of the appeal of the stamps to philatelists.

To raise capital I have already mentioned the issue of shares, and some companies have issued fixed-interest loan stock. Then there are grants and loans by official and other bodies, of which preserved railways could perhaps make greater use. The Development of Tourism Act 1969 authorized tourist boards to give financial assistance for projects which will provide or improve tourist amenities, and all three Welsh preserved railways have hopes of such assistance from the Wales Tourist Board. The Transport Act 1968 authorized both the Minister of Transport and local authorities to make grants towards capital expenditure for providing, improving or developing public passenger transport facilities. A contributor to the *Railway Magazine* (April 1968) suggests that these provisions enable local authorities to make grants to preservation societies to buy branch lines from British Railways. The Light Railways Act of 1896 makes extensive provision for financial aid to light railways. The Physical Training and Recreation Act 1937 authorized grants towards the expenses of voluntary organizations in providing facilities for physical training and recreation. The Lower Avon Navigation Trust, the members of which voluntarily maintain the locks, weirs and navigation works of the Avon in a manner comparable to a preserved railway, recently obtained a grant towards new landing stages under this Act. Railway preservation societies might usefully explore its possibilities.

The Transport Trust, a registered charity, aims to promote permanent preservation for the benefit of the nation of transport items of historical or technical interest, and also books, drawings, films and photographs of all forms of transport. It raises funds and puts them at the disposal of established preservation organizations, though where necessary it engages in preservation work itself. Several organizations connected with preserved railways are affiliated to the trust. The objective most likely to receive help from it is (at the time of writing) provision of proper covered accommodation for things already preserved. This appears to the council of the trust to be the most urgent need.

Most railways in Britain were built by railway companies. They developed distinctive styles of equipment—locomotives, coaches, signals, buildings. Throughout Victorian and Edwardian times there was a tendency for these companies to merge with one another. In 1923 railways were grouped, by government action, into four big companies: London, Midland and Scottish Railway Co., London and North Eastern Railway Co., Great Western Railway Co., and Southern Railway Co. Of these only the GWR had existed prior to the grouping—the other three were new creations. In 1948, railways were nationalized, to become British Railways.

Some small companies escaped grouping, and a few of these escaped nationalization. Such are the Talyllyn and Festiniog Railway Companies.

The expense of promoting railways by private bill caused hardship in rural areas in the nineteenth century by discouraging improved communications. To alleviate this the Light Railways Act 1896 was passed. It was reproduced in full in 1964 as an appendix to W. J. K. Davies's *Light Railways*. The Act enabled light railways to be authorized relatively cheaply by light railway order. The Welshpool and Llanfair Light Railway was originally so authorized and recently operating companies of preservation groups reopening closed British Railways branch lines have been granted L.R.O.s. These lines include the Bluebell, Worth Valley, Severn Valley and Dart Valley Railways.

Railways have also been built without statutory authority. Many of these were industrial railways—lines built by factories, quarries, etc., both for internal transport of materials and staff, and to give access to the main railway system at a private siding. Some owners of such railways who now use other means of transport allow preservation societies to operate them. In this category are the lines at Sittingbourne and Foxfield.

It is worth having a detailed look at the process by which closed lines of British Railways are preserved—that is to say, taken over and reopened as privately owned railways. The first step is for the preservation group to open negotiations with the British Railways Board. The board is prepared to entertain proposals from bona fide railway preservation societies, subject to approval of the Department of the Environment (which absorbed the Ministry of Transport in 1970). It also takes into account interests of local authorities and adjoining landowners. Obliged to pay its way, the BRB acts commercially: prices at which branch lines have been sold to preservation groups range between £5,000 and £10,000 a mile complete except for locomotives and rolling stock. Disposal in normally by sale rather than lease. Of the latter possibility, Mr. P. R. Dashwood, British Rail's chief estate surveyor (sales and purchases) was quoted in the *Financial Times* of 11 February 1972 as saying: 'If one of these [railway preservation] companies leased from us and failed to make a go of it, goodness knows what sort of a mess we would be left with.'

Negotiations with the BRB do not proceed far until it has received confirmation from the Secretary of State for the Environment that he has no objection to its disposing of the land on which railway and stations are built. Further, the board has agreed with the Department of the Environment to dispose of disused railway lines in the countryside so that, normally, they may be used as decided by the local planning authority. In urban areas, the board has an obligation to offer the land first to the local authority; if it is not sold, it may be offered on the open market.

Given agreement in principle so far, the next stage is to apply for light railway orders. Under the Light Railways Act 1896, L.R.O.s were at first granted provisionally by Light Railway Commissioners and confirmed by the Board of Trade—if both saw fit to do so. The powers of commissioners and board passed later to the Minister of Transport and are now exercised, under the original Act and later amending legislation, by the Secretary of State for the Environment. Just what a light railway should be was never defined. In practice, on railways built or operated under the Light Railways Acts, standards of construction and safety equipment have been relaxed, by comparison with main lines, in return for a speed restriction.

The 1896 Act is concerned mainly with new light railways—financing them and obtaining land—but it contains provisions for L.R.O.s both to enable existing railways to be worked as light railways and also for amending orders to alter or add to L.R.O.s granted previously.

So when a branch line is preserved two light railway orders are usually needed. The first authorizes the British Railways Board to work the line as a light railway and the second is an amending order which authorizes the preservation group or company to make an agreement with the board to purchase it, and transfers the line to its new owner on agreed terms with all the board's related rights, powers and liabilities.

Procedure of applying for a light railway order is governed by rules made by the Ministry of Transport in 1927. Applicants are advised to employ parliamentary agents to prepare their applications. Among many other requirements, notice of intention to apply for an order must be advertised in newspapers, and government departments have to be informed. The draft L.R.O. has to be deposited with the D.O.E. and local authorities, and also made available for public inspection. There is a fee of £50·00 to the D.O.E.

If the application attracts objections which are not settled by negotiation, a public local enquiry is held before an inspector who reports to the Secretary of State for the Environment. The application is then considered on its merits. Considerations include objections, safety of the public, financial resources of the applicant (for a railway without adequate finance is unlikely to operate safely), expediency of submitting the proposal to Parliament for a private act rather than a light railway order, and highway needs of the district. It is on the latter point, and in particular the costs which would be added to intended road improvements should they need to avoid or bridge the railway, that some L.R.O. applications have got into difficulty. But if all goes well the Secretary of State exercises his discretion and makes the order. It is then published by H.M. Stationery Office.

The second light railway order not only authorizes the preservation company to acquire and run its railway but also, I suggest, implies recognition by authority that the undertaking is in the public interest: that it is more than merely the whim of a few people to play trains.

Like any other statutory railway, the new preserved line has statutory obligations. Before it is opened for passenger trains it must be inspected and approved, in the interests of safety of its passengers, by an Inspecting Officer of Railways from the D.O.E.'s Railway Inspectorate. The Inspectorate operates under the authority of Acts of Parliament which promote railway safety. The first of these was the Railway Regulation Act 1840 and the most important subsequently the Regulation of Railways Act 1871 and the Road and Rail Traffic Act 1933. The Inspectorate has two main activities: inspections of new and altered passenger railways, and investigations of the causes of railway accidents. From the latter have originated many of the safety precautions demanded at the former. How they did so is described in L. T. C. Rolt's *Red For Danger* which is derived from the Inspectorate's accident reports and should be read and digested by anyone involved in running a railway.

Promoters of preserved railways are recommended by the Railway Inspectorate to approach them as early as possible, to discuss proposals and learn what the inspector will eventually look for. Points with which the Inspectorate is concerned include the purpose of the line, its length, stations and bridges, arrangements for long-term maintenance of bridges should the railway not prosper, motive power, operating arrangements, maintenance staff, insurance and a financial appreciation including capital outlay and an assessment of revenue and expenditure. Details of general requirements for signalling, track, stations, bridges, etc., including relaxations for light railways, appear in the Ministry of Transport booklet *Railway Construction and Operation Requirements for Passenger Lines and Recommendations for Goods Lines.*

Once open, the railway has to report accidents to the D.O.E. I hope it is not tempting providence too far to record that, at the time of writing, no accident has occurred on a preserved statutory railway that was severe enough to warrant an enquiry into its cause by the Railway Inspectorate.

So, running a preserved railway is something to be taken

seriously. But not so seriously that people forget to enjoy themselves.

A final point. The railways described in the next three chapters are in Wales, so place names are, mostly, in Welsh. Despite any appearance to the contrary, Welsh is an easy language to pronounce. It is almost always regular, which is more than can be said for English (Keighley? Leighton Buzzard? Buckfastleigh?), and it is pronounced as it is written. Difficulty only arises because certain letters and pairs of letters represent different sounds in Welsh from those they represent in English. The most important of these are:

Welsh	English (more or less)
ll	thl
dd	th (as in *th*ere; th, in Welsh, is always pronounced as in *th*anks)
ch	ch, always as in lo*ch*, not as in *ch*in
u	i, as in d*i*d
y	u, as in b*u*n, when near the start of a word, or i, as in d*i*d, when near the end of a word, or er, when by itself
w	oo
f	v ⎫
ff	f ⎬ (in other words, as in English o*f* and o*ff*)
au	i, as in w*i*ne.

With these, the knowledge that the last syllable but one is stressed, and some attempts I make to render names phonetically, readers should be able to tackle the Welsh names that arise without flinching.

2   The Talyllyn Railway

In February 1951 there appeared in *The Times* the following letter to the editor:

TALYLLYN RAILWAY

To the Editor of The Times

Sir,—The Talyllyn Railway, which runs for seven miles up a mountain valley from Towyn to Abergynolwyn in Merionethshire, is now the oldest surviving steam-hauled, passenger-carrying, narrow-gauge railway in the world. It is also among the very few independent companies surviving in the British Isles, established by Act of Parliament in 1865. The original locomotives and rolling stock are still in use. Following the death last year of Sir Haydn Jones, who was general manager and sole shareholder, efforts have been made to ensure that this historic railway shall not close.

To this end the Talyllyn Railway Preservation Society has been formed to raise funds and voluntary labour to repair the track and to maintain and augment the locomotives and rolling stock. Meanwhile the old railway company will continue in being on a non-profitmaking basis and will be administered jointly by representatives of the society and of the late Sir Haydn Jones. The society is relying upon wide support from the public in order to realize its ultimate aim, which is to make the Talyllyn Railway a living example of the old railway companies, as they were in the days before the amalgamation of 1921. Any inquiries or requests for further details should be addressed to the honorary treasurer of the society:

P. J. Garland, Esq. A.C.A., 36 Waterloo Street,
Birmingham.

Yours faithfully,
L. T. C. ROLT

Talyllyn Railway Preservation Society, 84 High
Street, Banbury, Oxfordshire, Feb. 17.

I knew the Talyllyn Railway—*Tal-er-thlin* as it is pronounced.
I had read about it, visited it, and then, two summers previously,
travelled on it. Trains ran three days a week and another visitor,
seeing it on a non-train day, expressed disbelief that so decrepit a
railway was actually in use. I returned and travelled. The ancient
0–4–0 tank locomotive *Dolgoch* hauled a train which consisted of
the railway's entire stock of passenger vehicles: four four-wheeled
coaches and a brake-van. The train ran over rails apparently held
together, rather loosely, by grass—it lumbered, lurched, jolted
and bumped. And, like all things less than full size, it was entirely
fascinating, for the track of the Talyllyn is but 2 ft. 3 in. gauge,
less than half the standard gauge, and locomotives and rolling
stock are in proportion.

I joined the society and one day in April 1951 returned to
Towyn for a brief visit. Throughout it, I recollect, *Dolgoch* stood
on the main line, such as it was, at Towyn Pendre station, raising
steam. No passenger trains had then been run by the society.
Close by, however, on the loop by which engines ran round their
trains, stood a train of six small and primitive wagons laden with
locomotive coal. Pendre is where the railway's locomotive shed
and repair works are situated, and the coal train had been hauled
thither the previous day from the terminus at Towyn Wharf where
there is an exchange point, for freight, with British Railways.

At the head end of the coal train stood a brake-van. 'We wanted
a pucka goods train, with the guard's van at the back,' explained
someone, 'but one of the wagon couplings is broken.' Further
down the line stood two more locomotives. I recognized both these
and the brake-van as having been obtained from the closed Corris
Railway, nearby, to augment the TR's own limited stock. *Dolgoch*
had dragged locomotives as well as coal trains from Wharf, and
very forlorn the locomotives looked after three years' disuse—rust

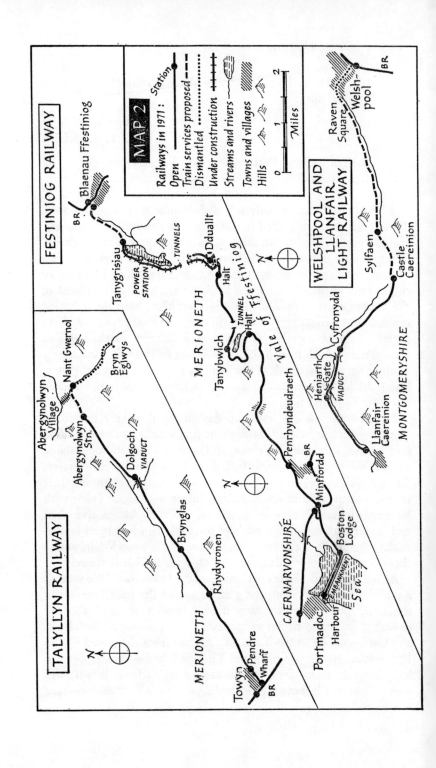

1 Old and new. Festiniog Railway double Fairlie locomotive *Earl of Merioneth*, on her last outing before withdrawal for preservation, stands on the Dduallt spiral at the farthest point to which track had been laid on the new Llyn Ystradau Deviation. The date is 31 Oct. 1971 and the train a special for delegates to the annual Festiniog Convention. (Author.)

2 Just like an ordinary train. But British Rail's last standard-gauge steam trains ran three years before this photograph was taken in September 1971 on the Severn Valley Railway. The class 8F 2–8–0 approaches Eardington, bearing a phoney number for filming. (Author.)

and grime were mingled with dark brown paint and their cab
windows were smashed.

From Towyn I went to Bala, by train. This was not, at that
time, anything remarkable. But since those days both the steam
trains I travelled in and much of the route they took have vanished
as completely as stage coaches and turnpike roads.

Reflect, for a moment, what Britain was like in 1951. The second
world war was certainly past, but the austerity which followed
was still present. Food had been rationed for eleven years and
would continue to be for another three. Prosperity and the
affluent society were not then in sight. Nor were motorways: the
term had not been coined, let alone any such roads actually built.
Travel by car meant a jog-trot along winding roads in a vehicle
which was, as likely as not, a twelve-year-old pre-war model.

In those circumstances railways generally seemed to have no
incentive to change or modernize. The big four companies and
most of the small ones had been nationalized three years earlier to
form British Railways, but there was little evidence of change.
Standard steam locomotives were being designed and built; diesel
multiple-unit trains, except for experimental units, were still in
the future. Local trains still ran on main lines, wayside stations
were still open and the bulk of the railway system was intact.
Only a few branch lines had closed in the thirties and forties from
bus competition. Sadly, these had included narrow-gauge lines of
great character.

Amateur enthusiasm for railways was concentrated around two
poles: construction and operation of model railways, and passive
interest in full-size ones—in locomotive performance, railway
history and photography. Boys collected engine numbers.

The author, still at school, regarded the latter activity with the
lofty disdain of one who has recently given it up.

Even in 1951, the Talyllyn Railway was an astonishing anach-
ronism. It retained equipment with which it had been opened 85
years before, a subsidiary of the Aberdovey Slate Co. That company had been set up by some Lancashire cotton businessmen.
When the American Civil War caused a shortage of cotton they
diversified their interests and attempted to exploit large reserves
of good quality slate supposed to exist at Bryn Eglwys, a quarry
in the mountains south of Abergynolwyn. The railway was built

R R—C

to carry the slate away; it was also to carry passengers and general goods.

Though small, the railway was well equipped for the period. Of other narrow-gauge lines which were slate quarry outlets, the Corris Railway still used horses to pull its trains, and the Festiniog Railway, 30 miles to the north, had replaced horses with steam locomotives and introduced passenger trains only a few years earlier. The Talyllyn was the first narrow-gauge railway to be designed for steam engines and passenger trains from the start. It was equipped with two locomotives, called *Talyllyn* and *Dolgoch*, three coaches—the fourth was soon added—and the brake-van; all were, then, of modern design. Wagons were provided for slate and goods.

Unfortunately the large reserves of Bryn Eglwys slate were not there; but purchasers rescued quarries, and railway, from closure in 1883 and again in 1910. Quarrying continued to a limited extent and railway equipment provided as a start to large-scale operation was more than adequate for small. The two engines, four coaches and brake-van were able to work all trains, with wagons added as necessary, and an increasing trickle of tourist passengers supplemented local travellers, goods and declining amounts of slate.

The purchaser in 1910 was Henry Haydn Jones, to be MP for Merioneth from 1911 to 1945. His purchase was motivated, probably, as much by philanthropy as profit. Certainly there was no profit left by the late 1940s; slate traffic on the railway ceased in 1947 as the quarry had closed. However, Sir Haydn Jones, as he had become, decided to keep the train service running for his lifetime. He was then in his eighties. No additions had ever been made to locomotives or carriages, and the original track was still in place, except for one short length which had been relaid. The once modern railway had gradually become a most remarkable antique.

In the summer of 1950, Sir Haydn died.

Prior to this, the idea of perpetuating the Talyllyn Railway had occurred to L. T. C. Rolt, engineer and author. Rolt had already pioneered public interest in veteran and vintage cars, and in inland waterways. In 1947 he was studying the text of the Transport Bill, the far-reaching measure to nationalize rail, road and water transport, to discover its effect on canals. From the list of undertakings to be nationalized he noticed a small omission: the Talyllyn Railway Company, forgotten, perhaps, by authority. Being also interested in railways he had visited the Talyllyn in the past.

Rolt regretted nationalization. It seemed to spell the passing of the *esprit de corps* which the old railway companies had manifested before they were grouped into the big four, and which the latter— particularly the GWR—had to some extent carried on.

In 1935 he had been a founder member of the Vintage Sports Car Club. There he had found a wonderful spirit which sprang from the practical activity of restoring, repairing and running vintage machinery. He reasoned that since railway enthusiasts lacked any such practical outlets for their interest and many had boring and uncreative jobs, they would welcome a creative task such as running a railway. This would help to make economical the venture of perpetuating the Talyllyn. The idea of such voluntary activity on a railway was entirely novel.

'Perpetuating' the Talyllyn, note, not 'preserving'. It was obvious that the line needed to be relaid throughout, which would, Rolt judged, be too costly even with voluntary labour. His scheme was to relay it as a miniature railway of $10\frac{1}{4}$ in. gauge. There was a precedent for this—in 1915 in Cumberland the Ravenglass and Eskdale Railway, then a worn-out narrow-gauge railway, had been relaid as a miniature railway. But Rolt did intend to keep Pendre as a museum to house the original locomotives and coaches. They would be run on mixed-gauge track which would be laid only from Pendre to Wharf.

Rolt at that time lived on board a canal boat and moored at Banbury for the winter. Through taking his radio set to be repaired at Trinder's Radio Shop in that town—from such insignificant actions do great movements spring—he came to know W. G. Trinder and the latter's friend J. H. Russell, both of whom shared Rolt's interests in canals and railways. He outlined his Talyllyn scheme to them; all three visited the railway during 1948 and 1949, and the scheme was discussed with Sir Haydn Jones. Sir Haydn saw the merit of the proposal but continued to operate the railway as it was.

Preoccupied with canals, Rolt was out of touch with railway enthusiasts generally. It was through J. H. Russell that he made contact with the railway enthusiasts' fraternity of Birmingham, and in particular with P. J. Garland and P. B. Whitehouse. It was these gentlemen who, after consideration, expressed the view that conversion of the Talyllyn to a miniature railway would not generate enough enthusiasm: only preservation of the railway in its then existing form would attract sufficient members and volunteers. Despite misgivings, for as an engineer Rolt was well aware of the railway's run-down state, he bowed to their judgment.

With the death of Sir Haydn Jones came the need for action. On 11 October 1950 a public meeting was held in Birmingham. The Talyllyn Railway Preservation Society was formed and a committee was appointed which included Rolt and his associates mentioned above.

They started negotiations with executors of Sir Haydn Jones. Fortunately, Lady Haydn Jones, Sir Haydn's widow who inherited the railway company shares, was most helpful. Rather than realize the value of the railway as scrap, she was prepared to let the society run it, without charge, for a three-year trial, and if the arrangement was a success it would become permanent. In February 1951 an agreement was made in which the principal points were that:

> Lady Haydn Jones would transfer all her shares in the Talyllyn Railway Co. to a new holding company to be called Talyllyn Holdings Ltd.;

> The Talyllyn Railway Preservation Society would raise funds by subscription to carry on operation of the railway;

> Directors of the Talyllyn Railway Co., and of Talyllyn Holdings Ltd. would be nominated as follows: two by Lady Haydn, two and the chairman by the TRPS.

This gave effective control of the railway company to the society.

The railway was valued at £1,350; should it close, this sum was to be returned to Lady Haydn.

Talyllyn Holdings Ltd. was formed as a company limited by guarantee. Its original directors were appointed for life, subject only to certain eventualities such as their resignation or bankruptcy, and its members, up to a limit of 25, were to be the original subscribers—founders of the society and Haydn Jones representatives—and such other persons as the directors admitted.

So the Talyllyn Railway survived the death of its owner and emerged from rural seclusion to become world-famous. The story of the early years of its revival inspired the film *The Titfield Thunderbolt* (although the actual filming was done elsewhere). The TR has seen far more change in 22 years of preservation than ever it did in the preceding 85 years. Reasons for change were twofold: firstly, most of the railway's equipment was worn out, so for the railway to survive at all, renewal was necessary; secondly, so popular has a ride on the Talyllyn Railway become with summer holiday-makers that the number of journeys made over it has increased from 5,235 in 1950 and 15,628 in 1951 to 159,981 in 1971. This has meant more and better locomotives and carriages, sound substantial track and improved stations.

But, much too, has not changed. The route remains the same. The hills and distant glimpses of the sea are as pleasant as ever. The line is still 2 ft. 3 in. gauge and still carries steam trains. And among all the innovations are still to be found running *Dolgoch*, much rebuilt but still entirely recognizable, her four coaches and brake-van. The society has remained faithful to rule three of its constitution, that it may not effect any change calculated permanently to alter the original character of the railway.

In 1971 trains ran on the TR from Easter until mid-October. The number of trains daily ranged from one each way, three days a week, in spring and autumn, to 11 or 12 each way, on Mondays to Fridays during the peak summer holiday season. The fare from Towyn Wharf to Abergynolwyn was 24p single, 35p return. There is a limited winter train service, described later.

Most passengers join Talyllyn trains at Towyn Wharf station. Officialdom now decrees that Towyn should be spelt *Tywyn*, but local tradespeople and the Talyllyn Railway continue to use the familiar spelling. Towyn—or Tywyn—is accessible by main road, with bus services, from Machynlleth, Aberdovey and Dolgellau. It has a station, a quarter of a mile from Towyn Wharf, on British Rail's Cambrian coast line. This line is under threat of closure but at the time of writing is still open. Through tickets can be bought to the Talyllyn stations of Dolgoch and Abergynolwyn from the BR stations of Barmouth, Pwllheli, Machynlleth, Borth

and Aberystwyth; they used to be available from many other
coast line stations before they were reduced to unstaffed halts.
On summer Sundays excursion trains, including those for mystery
destinations, run to Towyn from stations in England.

From Barmouth and many of the coast resorts the journey to
Towyn is quicker by rail than by road and even in these car-borne
days some 13 per cent of Talyllyn passengers come to Towyn by
British Rail. So seriously did the Talyllyn view proposed closure
of the coast line that it went to the expense of being represented
by counsel at the two public enquiries held by the Transport
Users' Consultative Committee for the area into hardship likely
to be caused.

Readers of *Railway Adventure*, Rolt's account of the first two
years of the TRPS, remember his mention of a large boulder
which lay at the Wharf Station, incongruous as a meteorite, but in
fact brought down from the quarry years before as 'an impossibly
weighty response to a request by a local lady for a rockery stone'.
There it had lain ever since, and there it still lies. It forms, at last,
the centre-piece of a small rockery, where its function is to protect
the awning above from damage by lorries entering the station yard.

There is not much else at Wharf unaltered. The layout of
the tracks had to be at first modified and then completely relaid.
The original two-roomed office building has been extended and
extended again so that it now forms the nucleus of a complex of
booking office, store, office, guards' room and shop. Passengers pass
through the Railway Shop on their way from booking office to platform. Here are displayed innumerable railway books, postcards,
transparencies, model railway components, and souvenirs: tea
towels, trays, charms, clothes brushes, rugs, wall plaques and pic-
tures, to mention only some of the most popular items.

Turning right on reaching the platform leads to the Narrow
Gauge Railway Museum. Here are static exhibits, many relics of
narrow-gauge railways both public and industrial. They range
from small items—nameplates, notices, signals—to complete
wagons and locomotives. The Narrow Gauge Railway Museum
Trust is a distinct entity, with its own membership. Trustees are
drawn from both the TRPS and other well known railway societies.

Signals are conspicuous by their absence on the Talyllyn. The
Department of the Environment remains satisfied that trains are

controlled safely by hand and flag signals. There is one exception: a colour light signal controls approach of trains into Wharf Station. Visibility is very bad, because of a long bridge on a curve, and people cross tracks in the station by a right of way.

The journey from Wharf to Abergynolwyn takes about 45 minutes. The railway runs north-east and may be divided into three parts. As soon as it leaves Wharf it enters a long cutting which continues for about one-third of a mile. Where it ends, sidings go off to right and left to locomotive shed, workshop and carriage sheds, and then follow the small platform and passenger shelter of Towyn Pendre. This station is more convenient than Wharf for the centre of Towyn. Soon after Pendre the line enters Snowdonia National Park and as far as Brynglas it climbs gently through open farmland with hills in the distance, although on the south side they come steadily closer. On this stretch are the station of Rhydyronen and several inconspicuous halts which serve farms.

At Brynglas the hills close in and shortly beyond the line starts to run, as it does for most of the rest of the route, on a shelf on the mountainside above a narrow valley. Clumps of gorse give way to woods of small gnarled oaks and the train rumbles through a couple of rock cuttings; suddenly there is a glimpse of a rocky torrent far below—the train is carried high above it by Dolgoch viaduct. Beyond is Dolgoch station with its rhododendrons.

Here there is a pause while the locomotive takes water and knowing passengers descend to photograph the operation. Others leave the train completely to visit Dolgoch Falls. Beyond Dolgoch the railway continues along the mountainside, past a quarry which has provided much ballast for its track, to Abergynolwyn station which is set among hills covered by attractive conifer woods. The stone-built station building, appropriate and old though it appears, was completed only in 1969. It includes a café and shop, and there is a picnic area at the foot of a short slope down which a lane leads to the main road and Abergynolwyn village half a mile further on.

The railway disappears out of sight round a bend beyond the station. This was the start of the 'mineral extension' to the slate quarry. Previously it was used by goods trains and now, after many years of disuse, it is being made good so that passenger trains may run along it—for it passes through the finest scenery on the railway. The land was purchased in 1964 and a light railway order has been obtained—the extension was constructed originally under way-leave agreements and was not covered by the Talyllyn Railway Act. Tight curves and steep gradients which were not intended for passenger trains are being eased and the track has to be relaid. The Wales Tourist Board has offered a grant of £8,330, that is 49 per cent of the cost, and by 1975, if all goes well, the terminus will be Nant Gwernol, more than half a mile beyond Abergynolwyn station. Here on a shelf on the side of a rocky tree-shaded dingle were once sidings, the limit to which locomotives worked. The extension continued to the quarry by steep inclines up which wagons were hauled by ropes.

The air of comfortable prosperity that the Talyllyn now wears gives no indication of the effort needed to achieve it. It has evolved gradually since 1951. Early years were touch and go—the trouble was the track. To earn revenue, more trains had to be run: as a result, the track was rapidly deteriorating to a point where it was no longer safe. There was a possibility that the railway would close. Escape from a vicious circle came through the efforts of the society's then chairman (and enthusiastic amateur locomotive fireman) the late Earl of Northesk. He pulled the strings for a Territorial Army unit to re-lay almost a mile of track as a training exercise.

Since then the whole line has been re-sleepered—a task which in 1951 seemed so formidable was completed seven years later—and re-railed: the last of the original rails in the main line were replaced in 1966. Second-hand materials were used: old sleepers from British Railways cut into halves, and rails from innumerable different sources. On sections recently relaid, new sleepers of Jarrah, an Australian hardwood, have been used. At £1·50 each they are three times as expensive as half-sleepers from BR, but are expected to last five times as long. The rail now laid weighs 50 and 55 lb. a yard and is stronger than is really warranted by traffic; and crushed granite ballast is used. With this substantial track, permanent-way maintenance, which loomed so large in the society's activities in the past, is expected to be minimal in future.

The locomotive story has been one of early additions to the stock followed by constant attention to keep locomotives running, and lengthy general overhauls to individual engines.

Locomotive No. 3 is an example. This was built in 1878 for the Corris Railway and given a new boiler in 1900; she was one of those I noted at Pendre on arrival in 1951. She was put into running order without much difficulty, although steam pressure was limited to 100 lb. per sq. in. because her boiler tubes were old, corroded, and unlikely to withstand higher pressures. She was repainted, named *Sir Haydn* in memory of the railway's former owner, and put into service. Unsatisfactorily. Track was wide of gauge, No. 3 had wheels with narrow treads, and she frequently came to grief, dropping between the rails. She was stored.

By 1953 the track had been improved enough for her to run regularly. In the winter of 1953–54 her boiler tubes were renewed and in 1954 she ran at a pressure of 135 lb. per sq. in. Towards the end of the season a small leak developed from a crack in the firebox. This was repaired by welding for 1955. To pass her for a further season the inspector then required heavy repairs and she was not used in 1956, but she returned to service in 1957 with a large steel patch riveted on to the firebox. In 1958 it became clear that a new firebox was needed, and the locomotive was withdrawn to await it.

By this time there were three other locomotives in service and more urgent matters received priority. It was not until 1961 that the engine was dismantled and examination showed that repairs would be so expensive that a new boiler and firebox would cost little more. The order was given to J. & W. Gower of Bedford— one of the few remaining firms able to build locomotive boilers. The boiler/firebox unit was delivered in 1964.

Meanwhile the rest of the locomotive had been examined. While the frames, driving wheels, axle-boxes and coupling rods, etc., were fit for further use, other components had to be renewed: cab, coal bunker, 'pony truck' in which the trailing wheels run, and hornblocks. The latter are castings bolted to the frames: the axle-boxes, in which the axles revolve, slide up and down in them while the weight of the locomotive is taken by the springs.

When new hornblocks had been fitted, the frames were lowered over wheels and axles. The axle-boxes were a very tight fit, and when an attempt was made to fit the coupling rods, it was found that the axles were not parallel. Everything had to come apart again and a check was made of dimensions. This revealed that the slots in the frames, to which the hornblocks are fitted, were $\frac{3}{16}$ in. farther apart on one side than the other! The original hornblocks had been individually made to compensate for this. By such methods were old steam locomotives built.

The new hornblocks had, not unreasonably, been made identical, and the axle-boxes now had to be modified to fit them. This was just one of many complications in rebuilding the locomotive. The new cab and coal bunkers, on the other hand, were built by Brush Electrical Engineering Co. Ltd., who had offered to help, as successors to Hughes who built the locomotive so many years before.

In 1966 the boiler and firebox were placed on the frames, but with staff and volunteers short and other stock to be maintained it was 1967 before rebuilding started in earnest. By August 1968 the locomotive was in steam for trials, and in September she entered traffic. She had been out of service for almost 11 years. Since the rebuild she has been found to be powerful and economical, and has required little attention. During 1970 she ran 3,573 miles, the most of any of the four steam locomotives in use.

Of the other locomotives, the boiler of No. 2 *Dolgoch* needed replacement by 1956 at a cost of about £1,500; it was 1962 before she returned to service, with a new boiler. The other original locomotive, No. 1 *Talyllyn*, had lain at Pendre worn out and out of use since 1946. She re-entered service, rebuilt and reboilered, in 1958; but by 1970 required another big overhaul.

Locomotive No. 4 *Edward Thomas*, from the Corris Railway, had been built in 1921 by Kerr Stuart & Co. Ltd. to a relatively modern design for industrial light railway locomotives. She was extensively repaired in 1952 by Hunslet Engine Co., successor to Kerr Stuart, and proved so useful in service that when her boiler was condemned after the 1962 season she was reboilered in time to be back in service in August 1964. From 1958 to 1968 she carried a Geisl ejector, a device to improve efficiency and economy. Locomotive No. 6 *Douglas* is another of industrial railway type, built in 1918. She was presented to the society in 1953, and altered to fit 2 ft. 3 in. gauge instead of 2 ft. for which she was built.

With these five steam locomotives, supplemented by various diesels used mainly for works trains, the TR has maintained its train service from 1951 until the present time. Seldom if ever have all five been operational at once, but the number available has steadily increased. By 1966 the need for an additional locomotive was evident and in view of the scarcity of suitable locomotives the exciting possibility of having a new one built was considered, and much thought and discussion went into its design. But in 1969, just as purchase of a new locomotive for some £12,500 was being considered, the railway was able to obtain a second-hand one, built only in 1950 and little used, from the Irish Peat Board for £300. However it was not, although basically similar to No. 6, a locomotive ready to run on the Talyllyn. For a start, it was for a gauge of 3 ft., with box frames incorporating a water tank that made it difficult if not impossible to narrow the gauge. Rather, this locomotive is regarded as a source of components for a new locomotive now being built. From the peat board locomotive come cylinders, boiler and firebox, driving wheels, axles and axle-boxes, and coupling rods, etc. Frames, cab, tanks and coal bunker are being made at Pendre, and there eventually the complete locomotive will be assembled as an 0-4-2 side tank. As for a name, when the peat board locomotive was delivered to Towyn, some wag with a taste for horrific puns chalked on her side *Irish Pete*; and *Irish Pete* was eventually the name officially adopted after a democratic process in which the society in annual general meeting considered and voted on six possibilities.

The stock of passenger coaches illustrates their evolution over 21 years. First to supplement the original coaches came open-air 'toast-rack' coaches which had carried quarrymen on the Penrhyn Quarry Railway in Caernarvonshire. None survives but there are several open-sided coaches with roofs, of design developed from the Penrhyn coaches. In the late 1950s, a search was made for bodies of suitable coaches which had been sold for sheds when the railways they ran on closed. Two from the Glyn Valley Tramway and one from the Corris Railway were obtained, and rebuilt and restored to their proper function. Subsequently a series of new and solid bogie coaches has been built, part of the work being done at Pendre and part by contract.

No continuous brake is fitted to Talyllyn trains, but they do have an electric alarm system which links locomotives, coaches and brake-van. It fails safe: should a train become divided, the circuit is broken so that a buzzer sounds on the locomotive.

Of the few goods wagons which were still in service in 1951, none survives in use today. Those which now run in works trains have been obtained elsewhere or built locally. An original slate wagon is exhibited in the museum.

To accommodate and maintain all the additional stock, installations at Pendre have had to grow. Carriage sheds have been repaired, built and expanded; the locomotive running shed has extended into what was formerly a cottage called *Railway View*. In the workshop alongside, only the forge and a hand screwing machine remain of the rudimentary equipment present in 1951. They have been joined by (among other equipment) lathes of two sizes, a half-inch drilling machine, a four-foot radial drill, a bench grinder, a shaping machine, a power hacksaw, two sets of welding equipment and a profile flame-cutter to cut steel plate to shape. It is now the most comprehensive engineering workshop for miles around and does work for outside customers in addition to the railway.

On the civil engineering side, a bad landslip occurred to an embankment near Dolgoch in November 1957. A culvert had become choked over the years and water had percolated the embankment. The culvert had to be dug out, cleaned and partly replaced, and a reinforced concrete retaining wall built to support the railway. It was usable, with a 5-m.p.h. speed restriction, in time for the 1958 season. By the winter of 1969, Dolgoch viaduct needed extensive repairs: scaffolding from the floor of the ravine, 20,000 bricks, 200 tons of sand and stone. The work was done by contract, and so much had the Talyllyn developed that it took the £4,000 cost in its stride.

One of the earliest actions of the society was to put in a telephone between Wharf and Pendre. The equipment was donated and installed by members. The telephone system has gradually been extended throughout the line. From Wharf to Brynglas the poles also carry wires for staff instruments—miniature electric train staff from Wharf to Pendre, and electric key token (the staffs look like large keys) from Pendre to Brynglas with its loop. The latter system is being installed from Brynglas to the next loop at Quarry Siding; from there to Abergynolwyn a train staff with detachable metal tickets is used.

Blockmen at loops set points, see that trains cross one another safely and report the times they do pass to a controller at Wharf, who records them in the train register book. With several trains on the move at once, the book provides an instant reminder of the latest reported position of any of them. The controller is in charge of operation of the line, with authority, for instance, to alter scheduled crossing places should a train run late. Before 1951, and for some years afterwards, one locomotive and set of coaches shuttling to and fro sufficed to carry the traffic; now, during the July and August peak, three trains are in use. In May and September, however, visitors can sometimes recapture the past when a special vintage train runs, with original locomotive and coaches.

The great majority of those who take a trip on the Talyllyn Railway are holiday-makers staying in the area bounded by Criccieth, Bala, Machynlleth and Aberystwyth, with Barmouth and caravan sites along the coast as the biggest sources. The busiest day of the week is Wednesday and the quietest Saturday, for on that day holiday-makers are arriving in the district or going home. People staying at a new caravan site near Rhydyronen use the railway to go to Towyn, and there is a very small amount of local traffic from this station, Brynglas and the halts to Towyn. For this, at various periods since 1951, winter trains have run on Fridays, usually hauled by diesel locomotives. In their latest form, the winter trains run between Pendre and Rhydyronen only. There is no commercial freight traffic, and parcels traffic, which survived in a small way in 1951, finally faded out during the 1960s. Railway letters are carried.

Traffic receipts increased from £704 in 1951 to £19,363 in 1970. The cost of operating the railway for a year increased during the same period from £970 to £18,924. The railway has other sources of income—the Railway Shop and catering—and other expenses, from rates and insurance to electricity and water. Until 1963 it functioned at a loss, made good by grants from the society. In 1964 it achieved a trading profit, and continues to do so. The profit is ploughed back.

The Talyllyn society was fortunate that it did not have to find a large capital sum to gain control of its line. With the notable exceptions of Lady Haydn Jones, and recently the Wales Tourist Board, there have been no big benefactors; restoration was paid for out of revenue, subscriptions and small donations, aided by occasional three-figure loans from members and an issue of 4 per cent unsecured loan stock by Talyllyn Holdings Ltd. which raised about £3,000 of working capital as and when this was needed. The society council of 20 members, elected at annual general meetings, is the policy-making body. Its chain of command towards the railway company should in theory start with instructions to the society-appointed directors on the company board. What in practice happens is that, by agreement, the railway company board deals largely with staff relations and legal matters while the society council deals with everything else.

Sub-committees appointed by the society council cover engineering, publicity, Railway Shop, and finance and general purposes; a further sub-committee, traffic and operating, comprises council members and elected representatives of volunteer firemen and guards. Additional sub-committees are set up from time to time for special projects, such as the extension to Nant Gwernol.

The railway company has three salaried officers; chief engineer, traffic manager and commercial manager, all of whom sit on the appropriate society sub-committees and attend council and board meetings (no paid staff may sit on the council). A director living locally mediates if they disagree.

As an instance of the workings of this system Talyllyn men, tongue in cheek, cite the question of the livery (nothing so mundane as a colour scheme for a railway locomotive) to be applied to *Sir Haydn* as the end of the 11-year overhaul approached. Except for the name of a locomotive, there is nothing that excites railway amateurs so much as the colour of the paint! Talyllyn engines are painted light green, and the coaches are crimson, with three exceptions. These are the historic Corris and Glyn Valley coaches, restored to the liveries of those lines. It was suggested that *Sir Haydn*, as an old Corris engine, might be restored to the red livery of that railway.

The subject first arose officially in the Railway Shop sub-committee. The shop would have to sell souvenir badges of the engine. The committee voted two members for red, two for green, the chairman's casting vote being for green.

Then the publicity sub-committee considered the publicity appeal of the two liveries. Its members voted three for red, three for green, but the chairman opted for red.

So the matter came before the council. On this important occasion all the backwoodsmen turned out. And after due deliberation the council members voted ten-ten! The locomotive's present green livery results from the council chairman's casting vote.

Membership of the society is divided into four areas—Southern, Yorkshire, Midlands and North-West, some of which have subgroups. Each member is automatically a member of the local area without additional subscription. Areas have their own committees, which organize working parties to the railway, publicity at traction engine rallies and similar functions, and meetings of members. The Southern area organizes a special train each year from London to Towyn for the society's annual general meeting.

Membership grew fast in early days—645 members by July 1951. Subsequently it had its ups and downs. In 1971 there were 2,811 members, and the number was slowly increasing. Adult annual subscription is £1·50 and members get free travel on Talyllyn and Festiniog Railways. Since the Talyllyn society no longer needs to subsidize the actual operation of the railway with cash, its main recruiting effort is for members who will help to run it.

Volunteers and paid staff together run and maintain the railway. The chief engineer has a paid staff of a dozen, including locomotive superintendent, drivers, fitters, track maintenance men and hedgers. The commercial manager has four assistants during the running season and the traffic manager two. The latter work as booking clerks, blockmen and guards, according to availability or otherwise of volunteers who do most such jobs. Running the three-train service employs up to 30 traffic volunteers. These are members who come to stay for a week or preferably longer.

Driving the steam locomotives, for long the preserve of permanent staff, was recently opened to experienced volunteers. There are only two volunteer engine-drivers so far, each of whom is able to spend a month's summer holiday on the railway. Fireman are usually volunteers. Much maintenance and construction work, from electrical wiring to carriage building, is done by weekend working parties of members from the areas. Some members have worked on the railway since the earliest days of the society. They have, however, a long way to go before they match the record of Edward Thomas. In charge of the railway under Sir Haydn Jones, and a director of the company from 1951, he retired in 1967 with the amazing total of 70 years' continuous service.

At the other end of the scale, much effort is put into training volunteers. Traffic seminars are arranged early each year at main centres of population. Experienced Talyllyn people show new and potential volunteers how the railway is run, with the aid of specially taken films and slides. At Towyn in summer are held mutual improvement classes, a traditional railwaymen's activity. Volunteers and staff from all departments get together to discuss, for instance, how to deal with a hypothetical emergency—say, failure or breakdown of a train between stations. There is talk of fitting out a building at Wharf as a training school.

On the engineering side, volunteers are taught specific skills, even welding, if they show aptitude and look like becoming regular visitors.

The Talyllyn Railway continues, preserved as a living organism, if such a thing is possible. Of necessity it caters for a lot of tourist traffic, but it endeavours to ensure that commercial development does not spoil its amenities and that it retains its friendliness and character.

3 Railway in Arcady. *The Earl*, on the Welshpool and Llanfair Light Railway, heads for Castle Caereinion in September 1971 with a train of coaches obtained from Austria. (Author.)

4 *upper* Winter snow. Bluebell Railway train hauled by P class o–6–oT
enters Horsted Keynes on Boxing Day, 1970. (Mike Esau.)
lower Summer day. Talyllyn Railway *Sir Haydn* approaches Quarry
Siding in 1970, after her 11-year overhaul. (G. F. Gillham.)

3 The Festiniog Railway

Strangely, some characteristics of railways persist when they are revived, despite changes in equipment and purpose. The Talyllyn, for instance, retains an appropriate minor railway atmosphere. The Festiniog, on the other hand, although it has a narrower gauge—1 ft. 11½ in.—and not much greater length of run—9½ miles—has a tremendous main line air.

Hamilton Ellis in *The Trains We Loved*, his delightful 1947 account of pre-1914 railways, identified it thus: '. . . at Minffordd Junction . . . the little Festiniog train with its double engine and low-down bogie carriages would come spanking in on the high level with all the air—and the particular noise—of a great express making a call by the way.'

Since 1914, the Festiniog Railway has seen years of decline, closure and gradual reopening, but today those words are as appropriate as ever. The railway is very busy: in 1971, 366,457 passengers made journeys on it, more than on any other preserved railway. In the whole of Wales the FR was exceeded in popularity as a tourist attraction only by Caernarvon Castle and the National Museum. Further, in the Festiniog Railway Society, with 5,600 members in 1971, the railway has the largest voluntary supporting organization of any line operating. The author, who has been a member of the society since 1954 and was a director from 1964 to 1972, is now trying very hard to write objectively!

The railway owes its popularity to three factors. Firstly, its route high among the mountains of North Wales is the most scenic, to use yet another superlative, of any preserved line. Secondly, rugged scenery combines with that main-line air to give the little railway its own specific fascination. Thirdly, it has history.

The Festiniog Railway's origin goes back to the early 1800s, when William Madocks built a mile-long embankment, at immense personal expense, to reclaim the Traeth Mawr estuary. It

R R—D

was finally completed in 1814. Existence of the embankment led
to establishment of the harbour and town of Portmadoc at its
western end; and, in due course, to construction of the railway.
The Festiniog Railway Company was incorporated by Act of
Parliament in 1832, during the reign of King William IV. This
company still owns and runs the railway, a remarkable example of
longevity. The original purpose of the line was to carry slate to
Portmadoc harbour (whence it was distributed in sailing ships)
from quarries around Blaenau Ffestiniog, some 13 miles to the
north-east and 750 ft. higher. *Festiniog* was spelt with one *F* in the
railway's act—spelling was not as standardized then as now—and
remains so spelt in the name of the railway. In the names of the
towns of Blaenau Ffestiniog and Llan Ffestiniog and of the Vale
of Ffestiniog the usual *Ff* appears.

When the railway was opened in 1836 it was not unconventional
for its period, though it would have seemed strange to our eyes.
The rails were carried on stone blocks for sleepers, and trains of
wagons for slate were pulled, on the level and up hill, by horses.
The railway was unusual in one respect: its engineer, James
Spooner, had taken advantage of the altitude of Blaenau to lay the
line out so that laden trains could travel down it by force of gravity.
Two and a half miles out of Blaenau is a ridge, which the line at
first crossed by rope-worked inclines; in 1844 the ridge was pierced
by the 730-yard Moelwyn Tunnel and the line ran continuously
downhill, on gradients from 1 in 144 to 1 in 70, from Blaenau
Ffestiniog to Boston Lodge at the east end of Madocks's embankment. It then ran along the embankment to reach Portmadoc.
Slate trains worked by gravity continued to run until 1940 and
even today gravity is found to be as potent as ever as motive power
for down maintenance trains. It surprises people waiting at level
crossings when a train comes flying through *without an engine*!

Like many Welsh valleys, the Vale of Ffestiniog has a more or
less level floor which terminates fairly abruptly among hills inland.
This feature presents no insuperable obstacle to roads and road
traffic, but the railway, to maintain its even grade upwards from
sea level, has to climb steadily along shelves cut on the steep
mountainsides until it is high above the valley floor. Fine and
extensive views are revealed to passengers—views which, as later
publicists were wont to point out, are unobtainable by any other

means. They attracted tourists to the line very early on: some form
of passenger conveyance was running for them as early as 1844,
and in 1859 the company's account books recorded a 'railway
carriage' valued at £12, '1 small do.' worth £6, and 'harness and
cushions of the company's passenger carriage', value £9 6s. 6d.

By then the slate trade was booming, James Spooner's son
Charles was manager, the track was being relaid and the railway
was approaching its first great milestone: introduction of steam
locomotives and steam-hauled passenger trains. At that period no
steam locomotive had been built for so narrow a gauge as 1 ft.
$11\frac{1}{2}$ in., and expert opinion held that to do so was impracticable.
Nevertheless, after many strange designs had been considered,
two small locomotives were built for the FR in 1863 by George
England & Co. They were a success. They were 0–4–0 tank
locomotives with tenders to carry coal—and indeed they still are,
for both, much rebuilt, still exist. Small four-wheeled carriages
were built, and, again, several from this period survive. After
inspection of the railway by the Board of Trade's inspecting officer,
passenger services commenced in 1865. All this was pioneering
stuff—for many years, since disputes between railways of standard and broad gauges, it had been illegal to construct new passenger railways of gauge less (or more) than 4 ft. $8\frac{1}{2}$ in., and the
Festiniog demonstrated the possibilities of narrow gauges.

Four more 0–4–0Ts followed quickly, but traffic grew quicker
still. By 1869 the company was considering doubling the line.
What it in fact did was to double the length of its trains by adopt-
ing double engines. These were built to Fairlie's patent, with a
double boiler (like two engines back to back with a chimney at
each end) mounted on bogies. The design produced powerful,
compact, locomotives able to traverse sharp curves. The FR's
first double Fairlie was built in 1869; the type had been tried
elsewhere but it was on the FR that its value was proven, and
examples survive there in use.

Overshadowed by double engines but perhaps more important
in the long run came bogie carriages—the first to be used in
Britain. The earliest were built in 1871 and these, too, are still in
service.

With a prosperous slate industry the Festiniog Railway also
prospered, and with all its developments became world-famous.

Narrow-gauge railways were built in its image in mountainous
regions from the Himalayas to the Rockies, Fairlie's patent double
engines were adopted in countries as far apart as Russia, Mexico
and New Zealand, and under-developed countries were opened up
cheaply and quickly by railways of less than standard gauge.

In 1889 came the death of Charles Spooner and the end of the
railway's connection with the Spooner family. By strange coincidence this is exactly half-way from its incorporation in 1832 to
closure in 1946. The railway coasted along for a while, then went
into slow decline. Both the Great Western and the London and
North Western Railway Companies had built standard-gauge lines
direct to Blaenau Ffestiniog, tapping the FR's slate traffic at source,
and carrying almost all the incoming goods traffic which had
previously come by coastal shipping to Portmadoc. The slate trade
out of Portmadoc harbour was dying away, but in 1872 exchange
sidings had been opened at Minffordd, two miles from Portmadoc,
between the FR and the new Cambrian Railways Co. standard-
gauge coast line. Some slate from Blaenau went that way. But
demand for slate as a roofing material was itself declining, as tiles
became cheaper. In 1912 the company paid its last dividend on
ordinary shares, and in 1921 its last dividend on preference shares,
according to the Stock Exchange Official Yearbook. In 1923, to
lessen working expenses, the company obtained a light railway
order for its line.

The tourist traffic, however, continued. In the 1860s, primitive
open-sided 'observation cars' had been introduced. A 1907 guide
book described the line's metamorphosis from horse tramway to
full-blown passenger line, remarked on the sensation this had
caused and commented that, *though the wonder had somewhat worn
off* (my italics), still no ordinary tourist visited Wales without
taking a turn on the 'toy' railway. Between the wars, as local
passengers deserted the trains for buses, tourists and holiday-
makers, and quarrymen, provided the railway with its passenger
traffic. After 1930 a full passenger train service ran only in summer;
winter passenger trains were limited to a train to take quarrymen
to work in the early morning and home again at night. In 1939, at
outbreak of war, all passenger services ceased. Subsequently, slate
trains ran between Blaenau Ffestiniog and Minffordd on three
days a week or less, and the line began to get into bad repair and

overgrown. By the end of the war the company had little traffic and few staff. It was unable to finance rehabilitation of the line for tourist traffic: on 1 August 1946 the railway was closed. It was not legally abandoned. The Ministry of Transport, though approached, had no powers to issue a warrant of abandonment for the Festiniog Railway. An Act of Parliament would have been needed. Whatever the legal position, the railway itself soon seemed all too literally abandoned. First grass and then bushes and brambles covered the track, saplings sprouted and grew into trees, and after a few years several miles of railway had disappeared under a jungle so thick as to be impenetrable even on foot.

The upper part of the line seems to have been less fertile, and remained passable. Indeed, residents of cottages beside it, who were otherwise isolated, took to running their own trolleys along the closed railway. A short section at Blaenau Ffestiniog remained officially in use, leased to slate quarries to provide them with a link to the standard-gauge stations. The quarries provided their own internal-combustion locomotives and operated this part of the line until 1962.

The dormant Festiniog Railway did not lack suitors. Stories of its imminent reopening became, I recollect, something of a hardy annual. From rents and the slate traffic in Blaenau the company still had an income. It also had big liabilities in debentures, loans and bank overdraft. When older and wiser people had investigated and, overcome by caution, withdrawn, it was left to 17-year-old L. A. Heath Humphrys to start the revival scheme that was eventually successful. The idea of a rehabilitation fund occurred to him early in 1950 and later that year he was in touch with the company. He was not then aware of proposals to preserve the Talyllyn. In September 1951 Heath Humphrys called a public meeting in Bristol, which was attended by 12 people, one of whom was A. G. W. Garraway, who later became and remains the railway's general manager. From this meeting originated the Festiniog Railway Society, although at the time the company would not let the name *Festiniog Railway* be used. Further meetings followed and in 1952 a full committee was formed. After examining the structure of the railway company the committee concluded that £3,500 would be required to gain control and a further £2,500 to start some sort of train service. This was long before the days when money flowed freely for such ventures. Public support, felt the committee, might provide the £2,500, but for the £3,500 a patron was needed.

Numerous private individuals and philanthropic organizations were approached without success until the committee made contact with businessman and devotee of railways A. F. Pegler (who was later to purchase the locomotive *Flying Scotsman*). He agreed to negotiate for control of the Festiniog Railway Company on the basis that he appointed new directors to it, that the society could see its way to raising a minimum of £2,500, and that company and society then work together.

A. F. Pegler was successful: control of the company changed hands on 22 June 1954 and he became chairman, as he remained until made president in 1972. It was agreed that the society would raise money for the company to resuscitate the railway and that Pegler would transfer his controlling interest to a trust. So that it could enter into a formal agreement with the railway company, the society was incorporated as the Festiniog Railway Society Ltd., by guarantee, in December 1954. The unincorporated Festiniog Railway Society remains technically in existence to cover junior membership and formation of area groups.

To jump ahead, a trust to hold the controlling shares was set up in 1955, and in 1956 a formal agreement was made between company, society and A. F. Pegler in which the main points were that: the company agreed that the society might use the name *Festiniog Railway* in its title; the company would devote funds received from the society for purposes of the railway; the society would enlist volunteer help; the company would give privilege travel to society members; and company and society would each be represented on the board of the other. As a result of the last point, one director is appointed to the society board by the company and one to the company board by the society. As for privilege travel, ordinary members go free third class and at cheap rates first class; life members get first class free travel. For several seasons it has been necessary to restrict members' privilege travel on the most crowded summer afternoon trains, but this restriction does not apply at present since the number of coaches has been increased. By reciprocal agreement members get free travel on the Talyllyn Railway.

In 1961 the society became a shareholder in the company, when it was issued with one hundred 5 per cent preference shares of £10 each in return for £1,000 which would otherwise have been the latest in a series of donations. In 1964 a new trust was set up and the controlling interest in the railway company transferred to it. This is the Festiniog Railway Trust, which is a registered charity. Its trustees, normally four, are drawn two from the company and two from the society and are appointed by A. F. Pegler. Objects to which its funds may be devoted include railway research, railway museums, assistance to railway apprentices and retired employees or their widows, and facilities for recreation and voluntary work on railways. The trustees are instructed to bear specially in mind charitable purposes connected with the Festiniog Railway. But no interest or dividends are paid on the investments which the trust holds in the railway company, so its income is extremely limited. In practice, it ensures that control of the company does not pass into undesirable hands.

Since 1954, other shareholders besides A. F. Pegler have given or sold their holdings to the Festiniog Railway Trust and its predecessor, and continue to do so from time to time. In 1971, the trust held around 60 per cent of each class of capital issued in the company: debentures, 5 per cent preference shares, 4½ per cent preference shares and ordinary shares. Of the minority shareholders, some are sympathizers, such as the society, and the author, who was issued with shares in return for providing the company with locomotive *Mountaineer* (I hasten to reiterate that no dividend is paid or likely). Many other shareholders cannot be traced, despite efforts. In the long years since the last dividends were paid, many changes of address and deaths of shareholders have not been notified to the company.

In 1970 the 1956 agreement was supplemented by a comprehensive 'declaration of common purpose'. This embraces company and society on one hand and society and its area groups on the other. It states that the objective of all parties is to restore, preserve and make prosper the Festiniog Railway, and then goes into formal detail about ways of achieving this objective.

Once the railway had changed ownership in 1954 the long task of restoration and reopening began. It is not finished yet. The task

began at the lower end of the line, for access was needed to the
railway works at Boston Lodge to overhaul equipment. By the
spring of 1955 the jungle had been cleared sufficiently for occasional
works trains, hauled by internal combustion locomotives, to run
up to Blaenau Ffestiniog. Then track was gradually cleared of
turf, patched up and relaid; locomotives and coaches were overhauled one after the other and rebuilt after years of disuse and
neglect; and buildings were slowly restored and renovated. The
railway has been reopened by stages. The passenger train service
was revived on 23 July 1955 over just one mile of route from
Portmadoc to Boston Lodge. Trains ran until the end of the
summer season and carried 21,786 passengers. In 1956 the train
service was extended for a further mile to Minffordd; in 1957 for
1¼ miles to Penrhyn; and in 1958, by great effort, for 4¼ miles to
the next station, Tan-y-Bwlch, 7½ miles from Portmadoc. Some
pronunciations: Minffordd, *Minforth* (th as *the*); Tan-y-Bwlch,
Tannerboolch (ch as in *loch*).

After 1958 came consolidation. Much track, for instance, had
only been patched, and needed complete renewal of sleepers and
ballast. Not until the Portmadoc–Tan-y-Bwlch stretch had been
brought into good condition did work start on the next section of
two miles to Dduallt (*Thee-athlt*). This was fully relaid before
being reopened. The first half-mile was dealt with in 1965 by
16th Railway Regiment, Royal Corps of Transport, as part of
training exercise *Shish Kebab*, which also involved operating the
Portmadoc–Tan-y-Bwlch stretch alongside the permanent staff
(good military experience, for there are still potential trouble spots
in remote parts of the world where communications are by unusual
railway). The remainder of the line to Dduallt was relaid by staff
and volunteers and reopened on 6 April 1968—not without a last-
minute rush. The previous winter an epidemic of foot-and-mouth
disease had broken out among farm animals along the Welsh bor-
der; to prevent its spread, travel through the area was severely
restricted, so volunteers could not go to the FR just when they
were most needed. Final adjustments were made to the track at
Dduallt station on opening day, before the first train; and for a
few weeks, until platform and run-round loop were complete,
passengers were unable to leave trains there.

The railway has not yet been reopened beyond Dduallt because

part of its course from there to the next station at Tanygrisiau
has been submerged by a reservoir for a hydroelectric scheme.
This is another reason why reopening to Dduallt was long de-
layed—for a time it appeared that a deviation route might have to
leave the existing railway below Dduallt, but in 1964 it was
decided that the deviation, now being built, would leave the old
line at the top end of that station.

The hydroelectric scheme—Ffestiniog Power Station, to give
it its correct title—is not without interest. It was the first pumped
storage scheme in Britain: that is, it has two reservoirs, one 1,000 ft.
higher than the other: water from the top flows down to the actual
power-station to generate electricity and passes to the lower
reservoir. When demand is slack, spare electricity from the grid
is used to pump water back up to the top reservoir again. As the
scheme is within the Snowdonia National Park, much attention
was paid to amenities: the Central Electricity Generating Board
suggests that the power-station itself is the largest building constructed of local stone since the mediaeval castles of Harlech and
Criccieth.

The scheme originated in 1951, when proposals for an ordinary
hydroelectric scheme were announced just after the embryo
Festiniog Railway Society started negotiations with the company.
The proposals were later dropped—but revived as the pumped
storage scheme, which was eventually authorized by the North
Wales Hydro-Electric Power Act, 1955, although the FR Company
had petitioned the Select Committee of the House of Lords against
it, in March and April of that year. At that time the company had
changed hands and intended to reopen its line, for it expected
(and still expects) much holiday traffic via Blaenau Ffestiniog from
popular north coast resorts. But no passenger trains had run for
16 years and the company had neither reopened any of its line nor
demonstrated its ability to do so. It sought an amendment so
that either the electricity works would be altered to avoid flooding
the line or a deviation railway, including a tunnel, would be built
at public expense. Their lordships weighed probables (six-figure
cost) against possibles (reopening was no foregone conclusion)
and, 'with very great regret' declined to accept the amendment on
the ground of expense. In 1956 the electricity authority was able
to enter the railway company's land. The remaining $1\frac{1}{2}$ miles of

line from Tanygrisiau to Blaenau Ffestiniog became detached
from the rest of the railway.

The railway company was, of course, to be compensated. It has
taken a long time to establish the amount of compensation. At a
hearing by the Lands Tribunal in 1960 the company claimed that
compensation, in accordance with one of the rules by which
compensation may be assessed, should be based on the cost of
reinstatement of the line, then estimated at £180,000. The Lands
Tribunal decided that it should not. An appeal by the company
against this decision was dismissed in 1961 by the Court of Appeal.
Perseverance was rewarded in 1971 when, after a further hearing
by the Lands Tribunal, the company was awarded £65,000; the
bulk of the award is for loss of profit (the company having for
many years produced an operating profit which is ploughed back)
between 1962, when it was accepted that the line could have been
reopened to Blaenau had it not been flooded, and 1977, when it
was estimated that it would be reopened using the deviation route
which is being built. Interest since 1956 increases the sum awarded
to about £100,000—but it is not enough to pay for the deviation.

In 1971 the railway continued to run between Portmadoc and
Dduallt. Its station at Portmadoc, called Portmadoc Harbour, is
at the east end of the town. There is a small car park adjacent and a
larger one nearby, and bus stops nearby also; but the British Rail
station is over half a mile distant. The FR's summer operating
season has lengthened steadily over the years so that in 1971 'summer' extended from 13 March to 28 November. At ends of the
season there was but one train each way on Saturday and Sunday
afternoons only, but at the peak (spring bank holiday week and 10
July to 3 September) there were up to 13 trains each way a day.
At intermediate periods there were services of three trains a day
or more appropriate to the traffic. Like the length of the season,
the number of trains daily has gradually increased over the years.

Journey time from Portmadoc to Dduallt is about 50 minutes
each way. The adult return fare in 1971 was 70p third class, or
£1·00 first, with reductions for off-peak trains, such as those in the
evening, or out of the main holiday season. Early afternoon trains
in summer tend to be crowded. At Christmas time, special trains
run, and Father Christmas meets them at Dduallt with presents
for young travellers. Each FR passenger train includes a licensed

buffet car and an observation car. The latter runs at the Portmadoc end of the train: extra large windows in sides and end
enable passengers to observe scenery on the way to Dduallt and
the locomotive on the way back.

Portmadoc Harbour station has tea bar, book-and-souvenir stall,
a small museum of exhibits from the FR's historic past and a
public address system. Trains run along the top of the Traeth
Mawr embankment, called the Cob, when they leave the station,
and soon pass from Caernarvonshire into Merioneth. There are
fine views to Snowdon on one side and the sea on the other. At
Minffordd, the FR passes above British Rail's Cambrian coast
line by a bridge—stations are connected by a short subway.
Through tickets to FR stations from coast line stations have been
withdrawn since most of the latter became unstaffed halts; but
BR issue runabout tickets in conjunction with the Great Little
Trains of Wales. Tickets cover the coast line, the FR and other
lines such as the Talyllyn and the Welshpool and Llanfair.

Shortly before Penrhyn the line takes up the hillside shelf
formation which it follows for most of the rest of the way to
Dduallt. Penrhyn station buildings are now a well-equipped hostel
for volunteers working on the line. After Penrhyn the railway
enters Snowdonia National Park; after a further mile comes Cei
Mawr, the highest of many remarkable embankments made by dry
stone walling techniques. Wooded hillsides follow—before leaves
come in spring, this stretch offers the finest views (in the author's
opinion), back down the Traeth Bach estuary with Harlech
Castle in the distance. Tan-y-Bwlch station is the head of a more
or less horseshoe-shaped re-entrant with a lake among the
woods far below; the station is accessible by the steeply graded
B4410 road and has car park and café. Through tickets are available from stations on the north coast of Wales to Portmadoc, by
train to Blaenau, bus to Tan-y-Bwlch and FR train onwards.

Between Tan-y-Bwlch and Dduallt are the most spectacular
precipitous stretches of the FR, and also a short tunnel. Campbell's
Platform serves Y Dduallt manor nearby; not far beyond the railway reaches Dduallt station. There is no road to it—access other
than by train is only over indistinct public footpaths. There are
picnic site and view point.

At the top end of Dduallt station the line splits. One line goes straight ahead, the other bears round to the right. The former, now a grass-grown siding, was the commencement of the old route to Blaenau; the latter is the commencement of the new. In 1962 the company, undismayed by having lost its appeal against the first Lands Tribunal decision, decided that somehow or other it would still reinstate its line to Blaenau Ffestiniog. The old line had run more or less direct from Dduallt, climbing steadily through Moelwyn Tunnel to reach the floor of an upland valley from which it continued to rise to Tanygrisiau. This valley was flooded to become the lower reservoir, Llyn Ystradau, and the top end of the tunnel, which would have been below water level, was plugged. Any deviation must rise sufficiently high to clear Llyn Ystradau. The most direct route is then along its west shore, but this was obstructed by the power-station building and opposed by the Central Electricity Generating Board. Two surveys, both involving long and expensive tunnels through the ridge between Dduallt and Llyn Ystradau, had already been made.

In 1963 another survey was made by civil engineer and society member Gerald Fox, assisted by volunteers. The following year the results were announced—the highly original plans for the Llyn Ystradau Deviation. The new route started from Dduallt station (and so made it worthwhile to reopen the Tan-y-Bwlch–Dduallt section). It swung round in a spiral to climb back over the existing line by a bridge where it enters the station and continued, to parallel the old route farther on but 30 ft. higher. By this means the proposed line gained enough height not only to rise above Llyn Ystradau but also to avoid long tunnels; it ran along the east shore of the reservoir and crossed its dam to gain Tanygrisiau. The company applied for an amendment order to its light railway order of 1923 to authorize this route, or most of it—the final stretch over the dam was left for later. After a public local enquiry the order was made early in 1968.

In the meantime the first piece of land needed had been given to the company and construction had commenced in 1965. The manner in which the deviation is being built is as original as its design and derives equally from Gerald Fox who became the first project engineer. It is, almost entirely, a voluntary project, and as such is surely unique. Only in 1971 was a permanent staff site foreman appointed, himself a former volunteer. Most of the work is shifting rock from cuttings to make embankments. At each working site rock is first blasted, under strict and skilled supervision, to loosen it. It is then loaded into skips, or tipper wagons, which are pushed along temporary track to the embankment end of the site where the rock is dumped. Slowly but surely sites extend until they are linked. A small excavator and two small dumpers help where the terrain is suitable. Then, in addition to cuttings and embankments, there are bridges, culverts and stone walls to be built.

Volunteer diggers—male and female—who come to the deviation have varied backgrounds, though many are young professional people and many, too, have no specific interest in railways. A constructive weekend of physical exercise among the mountains is a valuable antidote to city tedium. Some come for longer than a weekend, and in summer work-camps are arranged. With two messes, close to the deviation, in which volunteers stay, it has its own social life.

In 1971 the Central Electricity Generating Board relented and allowed the railway to be routed past the back of the power-station. This means it can take the short route along the west shore of Llyn Ystradau, and though a tunnel is needed through the ridge, it is to be only about 311 yards long because the railway will have gained height by the spiral. Work already done on the deviation is usable. The west shore route has been surveyed and adopted, and application is being made for a further light railway amendment order.

By this route, the total length of new railway to be built is 14,367 ft. At the end of 1971, the formation was complete for 2,800 ft., and track had been laid over 2,200 ft. of this, by permanent staff and volunteers. Work was in progress on the formation of over another 6,700 ft. So far, 25,000 tons of spoil have been moved, with another 45,000 or so to come, plus the tunnel. Seven out of thirteen culverts for streams and 'creeps' for sheep to cross the line have been built; and Rhoslyn Bridge, by which the new line, on its spiral, crosses over the old, is complete. There are two other principal bridges, which are being designed; these and the tunnel will probably be built by contract. This leaves plenty for volunteers to do—and the amount of work done voluntarily increases year by year. Up to the end of 1971, the cost to the company, with capital

invested in plant, etc., was about £15,000; an engineer's rough esti-
mate of the cost of having the same work done by contract is
£60,000.

Between Tanygrisiau and Blaenau Ffestiniog, a limited pro-
gramme of repairs to trackside walls and ditches has already started.
So far as the part of the line in use is concerned, the story of the
Festiniog Railway in the second half of the 1960s closely parallels
that of a century earlier: rapid increase in traffic has led to improvements and additions to locomotives, rolling stock and track.
By 1971 the railway had five steam locomotives in operation. Two
of these were double Fairlies—*Earl of Merioneth* and *Merddin
Emrys*, built at Boston Lodge in 1886 and 1889 respectively. Two
more, *Linda* and *Blanche*, had been obtained from the Penrhyn
Quarry Railway in the mid-1960s, having run there since they were
built by the Hunslet Engine Co. in 1893. Both were originally
0–4–0 saddle tanks, and both have had tenders added at Boston
Lodge to carry fuel and extra water; *Linda* has been converted to a
2–4–0 which makes her ride more smoothly. The fifth locomotive,
Mountaineer, arrived on the FR in 1967. She is a 2–6–2T built
in 1917 by the American Locomotive Company for the British
War Department to use on military light railways in France; after
the first world war she was sold. She ran on the *Tramway de
Pithiviers à Toury* from 1935 to 1964, when that line closed. The
locomotive was then in danger of being scrapped, but being both
of historic interest and, what is more, of a design suitable for
hauling passenger trains, she was purchased by the author, with
the assistance of the *Fédération des Amis des Chemins de Fer
Secondaires*, and brought to England. Total cost, including transport, was about £800. She now belongs to the FR Company, with
the proviso that should it wish to dispose of her it should obtain
my approval.

Locomotive *Prince* is one of the 1863 originals, and was probably
the first locomotive to see a century of service. In 1971 she (he?)
was having a long-term overhaul. These six locomotives, which
all belong to the company and are painted in its green livery, are
the only steam locomotives to have hauled passenger trains since
reopening. There are also several small diesels which occasionally
see passenger use but are normally reserved for works trains; and
there is a further steam locomotive, blue 0–4–0 saddle tank *Brito-*

mart which came from a slate quarry and was restored by her owners, a syndicate of staff and volunteers. Too small to haul trains, she is sometimes seen shunting carriages for her owners to service them.

Four other steam locomotives await rebuilding. Two are Festiniog o–4–os of the 1860s; the third is an o–6–o saddle tank, dating only from 1944, which needs modification, and the fourth is No. K1, the original Beyer Garratt articulated locomotive built in 1909 by Beyer Peacock of Manchester for service in Tasmania. As the first of an original and highly successful design, she was repurchased by her makers many years after the line she ran on had closed, and brought home. When Beyer Peacock in turn closed down, she was bought by the FR for £1,000. The FR has been adding potentially useful locomotives to its stock as the opportunity arose. While increasing traffic has demonstrated the need, sources of supply have steadily become rarer.

The railway also modifies and rebuilds its existing locomotives to improve their performance. Biggest exercise in this respect has been provision of new boilers for both double Fairlies. The boilers were built by Hunslet Engine Co.; *Merddin Emrys* was rebuilt with her new boiler in 1970, *Earl of Merioneth* in 1971–72. In the latter instance, so much of the old locomotive needed replacing that the result of the rebuild will in effect be a new locomotive carried on the bogies of the old. The bulk of the old locomotive, on the other hand, is being preserved, as the only FR Fairlie to survive with appearance basically unchanged since the railway's heyday in the 1880s.

Since 1970 most steam engines have been converted to burn oil fuel instead of coal. This is more economical, simplifies handling, improves performance and avoids difficulties over supply of suitable coal. Above all, it virtually eliminates fire damage from sparks in the many forestry plantations alongside the line.

Passenger train vehicles in 1971 comprised 18 bogie coaches, two tourist cars, five four-wheeled coaches and two vans. When the railway was taken over in 1954 its coaches had not been used for fifteen years. Some were stored under cover, some were in the open and some were in a shed of which the roof had collapsed on top of them: much of their woodwork was rotten and a few were beyond repair. To restore and rebuild the others has been a long, gradual and painstaking process. Of the coaches in use in 1971, ten bogie coaches and the five four-wheelers were on the railway in 1954. Since that date, two coaches built for other railways long since closed have been obtained and rebuilt after long periods spent as hen-houses, and six new bogie coaches have been built at Boston Lodge, using parts made by contract. They are open saloons, with corridor connections. In theory they seat fewer people than the old coaches with separate compartments, but in practice they are more satisfactory. For instance, when trains are crowded, family parties of three or four adults and children do not like to be split up into separate compartments, but happily occupy vacant seats in a saloon coach. Two tourist cars, the first of several, simple open-sided coaches intended to carry peak crowds, were built at Boston Lodge in 1971, using underframes and bogies from similar coaches of the 1920s. Livery of coaches is cherry red with black ends.

There are about 180 wagons (the old FR had six times as many). Some are former slate wagons adapted to carry materials and equipment for maintenance, others are recent additions to the stock.

Locomotives and rolling stock are overhauled and maintained at Boston Lodge Works, as they have been for over a century. Much equipment new to the works has been installed since 1954, often obtained advantageously through well-wishers. Earlier equipment which is still used includes planing and slotting machines and a wheel lathe in which pairs of wheels on their axles are machined to correct worn treads and flanges. Steam railway maintenance is specialized so the works aims to be as self-sufficient as possible and can now do most jobs necessary except boiler manufacture. An example of something the works cannot yet do— there are thoughts of installing suitable equipment—is to make replacement springs for locomotives and coaches. Four or five have to be renewed each year. But spring manufacturers prefer orders to be in thousands—so a new spring for *Linda* or *Blanche* costs £40·00 with 15 months for delivery.

At Boston Lodge, versatility is the keynote. Staff and regular volunteers, though specialists in one or two jobs, are competent at others. This means for instance that a specialist in machining components knows enough about welding to make up any jigs he

5 *upper* Timeless scene. Isle of Man Railway: 2–4–0T *Kissack* and train hurry down the grade from Santon in August 1971. (Author.)
lower Sad occasion. Dart Valley Railway on 2 October 1971, first and last day of trains to Ashburton. (Author.)

6 *upper* Largest locomotive. A4 class *Union of South Africa* and observation car leave Lochty station. (Lochty Private Railway Co.)
lower Smallest railway. *River Esk* and train arrive at Dalegarth terminus, Ravenglass and Eskdale Railway. (Author.)

may need. As usual with factories and works, Boston Lodge is not open to the public. But reasonable requests to the works manager for permission to look round are seldom refused. Visitors' attention is then drawn, if necessary, to hazards such as fresh varnish or wet concrete; and pilferage of souvenirs, from which the works has suffered excessively, is minimized.

Condition of the track has steadily improved. All sleepers in the main line of the railway in use have been replaced, many of them by new sleepers of Jarrah. Much rail has been replaced by old but less worn rail from the Penrhyn Quarry Railway, and many joints between rails are, following up-to-date practice, welded. Most of the ballast is new, and many miles of lineside fences have been restored.

The railway's private automatic telephone network is by a long way the most ambitious and extensive on any preserved railway. It has five exchanges with 'narrow-gauge railway trunk dialling' and caters for 140 telephones, of which 87 were connected by 1971. Installation is to Post Office standards. The first automatic exchange came into use in 1965 after the omnibus telephone system used since reopening had become overloaded—though it is still maintained and used.

The railway is operated by the electric train staff system. It was formerly equipped with a miniature E.T.S. system: the instruments have been reconditioned and brought back into use along with others purchased from British Railways. The principal passing places are Minffordd and Tan-y-Bwlch. Subsidiary instruments are provided at Boston Lodge, Penrhyn and Campbell's Platform—all places in sections where non-passenger trains sometimes get clear of the main line. 'Remote operator' equipment enables a staff to be extracted from an instrument when no-one is on duty at the far end of its section. Trains sometimes pass one another at the loop at Penrhyn: for this purpose separate instruments are brought into use for the short sections Minffordd to Penrhyn and Penrhyn to Tan-y-Bwlch. Colour light signals are used at Minffordd, Penrhyn and Tan-y-Bwlch, and semaphores at Portmadoc and Dduallt.

Movements of trains are regulated by telephone from a control office at Portmadoc. This is now manned throughout the year, though outside the main summer season the controller doubles

with another function, such as booking clerk. The controller
marks movements of trains, as they are reported to him, on a graph
which shows time against distance along the line.

During the summer almost all the Festiniog Railway's passengers are holiday-makers staying in north-west Wales, and surveys
indicate that 75 per cent of passengers visit Portmadoc specially
to ride on the railway. Trains are busiest when the weather is dry
but too cool for lazing on the beach: both wet and hot sunny
weather bring fewer passengers. About 1,000 visitors a year use
the through rail and bus bookings from north-coast resorts,
despite the inconvenient journey. At the ends of the season weekend visitors to the region become important. There is a little local
passenger traffic between Penrhyn and Portmadoc, and there is
occasional freight or parcels traffic—usually fuel or furniture to
isolated houses near the line, though in 1970 a load of timber was
carried from Portmadoc to Tan-y-Bwlch. There is a railway letter
service.

In the long-ago 1955 season, receipts from passengers were
£440 and there was a profit on goods sold of £262. Expenditure
on the railway for the year was £3,487. In addition to running
costs and current maintenance, this figure included deferred
maintenance, that is to say the cost of work done during the
year towards making good many years of neglect and disuse.
That year the Festiniog Railway Society contributed £574 to the
company.

By 1962, passenger receipts for the year had increased to £13,612
and profit on sales was £1,305. The figure for maintenance
expenditure was split: current maintenance was included in
operating expenditure to total £9,022. With some miscellaneous
receipts, the operating profit was £6,151, which was put towards
deferred maintenance. The society provided £1,603.

In 1970, passenger traffic receipts (which include fares, car park
fees, platform tickets sold as souvenirs and the railway letter
service) were £66,650 and the profit on sale of goods and refreshments was £8,757. Operating expenditure was £48,318; after other
expenses, the profit for the year was £24,794. As usual it was
ploughed back. In the year ended 30 September 1970 the society
produced £3,827 for the company. The society's contribution is
valuable because of its timing; much of it comes in spring, when

subscriptions have been renewed, and the company faces expenses of preparing the railway for the coming season without having received much income since the last.

The railway's administrative chain of command is from its board (where each director, though responsible for a particular sphere of activity such as motive power or publicity, is non-executive) through the general manager to heads of departments. There are six departments: Traffic and Commercial (which includes catering and sales); Works (which includes mechanical engineering and building); Permanent Way (which includes track, lineside walls and bridges); Signal and Telegraph; Electrical; and Road Transport (the company's lorry). Some heads of departments are paid staff, some are honorary. They meet together about once a month. Going up the scale, each department proposes annual programmes of work, with costings. These are discussed at a management meeting so that the general manager can prepare a budget for submission to the board each November.

Work on construction of the deviation is administered by the company's Civil Engineering Department (New Works), responsible to the board; but track is laid on completed formation by the Permanent Way Department.

There are two joint committees with members drawn from boards and officials of both company and society. These are the Joint Publicity Committee and the Joint Committee on Preservation. The latter includes the honorary curator of the company's extensive archives and endeavours to reconcile preservation of historic equipment with operation of a very busy railway.

The Festiniog Railway Society has a board of twelve directors which meets bi-monthly; additionally, joint meetings of the boards of both company and society are held twice a year. Detailed management of the society is the province of a Management Committee which meets once a month under the managing director. A Group Sales Committee has been set up to arrange purchase and distribution of goods for re-sale by the society's area groups. Adult annual subscription to the society is £1·50.

The society has 12 area groups of which the farthest from the railway is Hants and Sussex and the nearest are North Staffordshire, and Lancashire and Cheshire. Each has its own committee elected by its members. Every autumn a Festiniog Railway

Convention is held over a weekend, attended by people involved in running railway, society and groups.

The permanent staff of the railway has grown from one in 1954 to 41 full-time and four part-time in 1971; with temporary staff the figure rises to a peak of about 70 in high summer. Most permanent staff, including all salaried staff, started as volunteers. During the course of a year about 400 individual volunteers, mostly society members, work on the railway, with a maximum of about 80 present on one day. Volunteers are to be found at all levels throughout the organization, according to their skills, training and experience. As the railway grows, so does the need for volunteers. Most of them either come to stay for a week or more in summer, or visit the railway at weekends throughout the year, often in working parties organized by the area groups. The appeal of the FR is strong enough to attract weekend working parties from as far away as Hants and Sussex, and London.

'Homework' by group members is extensive and ranges from production of notices and litter bins to overhaul of wagons and construction of a new brake-van. Group members also attend functions such as traction-engine rallies in their areas, with stands to publicize the railway and sell books and goods on its behalf. Among the latter are souvenirs with traction-engine motifs produced specially for the purpose. A project which originated with the London Area Group was production of *The Volunteers' Manual*. The second edition, published by the society, is a 32-page illustrated guide for those working on the Festiniog Railway.

Two further examples indicate the ramifications of FR activities. It has produced, largely by voluntary effort, a comprehensive range of drawings and parts for models of the railway and its equipment. And on the catering side, in 1971, customers ate 51,000 ices, 10,000 Mars bars, and 7,000 fruit pies; these they washed down with 2,000 gallons of beer, 1,270 gallons of orange squash and 17,000 cans of Coca-Cola.

Figures to do with the Festiniog Railway tend to come with a lot of noughts on the end now, and look like having still more in future. Company and society have plans.

4 The Welshpool and Llanfair Light Railway

Many preserved railways are operated under light railway orders, but only the Welshpool and Llanfair resembles the sort of railway envisaged by nineteenth century protagonists of light railway legislation. It was built for just the purpose they intended: to provide cheap transport, in times when transport meant rail transport, in a rural agricultural area; and it was authorized by one of the first L.R.O.s made, in 1899.

The railway's transport function has vanished, but other light railway characteristics—and charm—remain: narrow gauge (2 ft. 6 in.), sharp curves, steep gradients, undulating course with few deep cuttings or high embankments, level crossings without gates across the road, pastoral surroundings and a terminus at a quiet country town.

Since the railway is neither in a holiday area nor close to big cities, it is not swamped by hordes of visitors. Original locomotives and stumpy Austrian light railway coaches can be appreciated in authentically uncrowded conditions.

The railway is operated by Welshpool and Llanfair Light Railway Preservation Co. Ltd. It starts from a terminus adjacent to main road A458 at Llanfair Caereinion, Montgomeryshire. Here are shop, tea bar and small car park; when crowds do come, a field is used also. The railway runs eastwards, down the valley of the Afon Banwy, crosses this river by a viaduct, and then ascends the valley of a tributary to Castle Caereinion. Castle is 4¼ miles from Llanfair; there are intermediate stations at Heniarth Gate and Cyfronydd.

The countryside is hilly without being bleak. Gentle slopes, woods and meadows combine with placid cattle, grazing sheep and harvest fields of corn to make an Arcadian scene.

Beyond Castle Caereinion the line continues. As I write, restoration work proceeds on the track as far as Sylfaen, just over a mile, with the object of reopening this section in July 1972. This will give a terminus on a main road—the same A458—at the eastern end of the line. It is from the east that most visitors approach. From Sylfaen the line, out of use, continues further. It descends Golfa incline to Raven Square, at the west end of Welshpool and just over eight miles from Llanfair. Part of the descent, a mile at 1 in 29 and 1 in 30, is in railway terms very steep. Beyond Raven Square the line used to continue, by many ungated crossings and an intricate winding course between the houses, to Welshpool standard-gauge station on the far side of the town. This section is closed and mostly dismantled.

In 1971, trains ran from Easter to the end of September, daily at the most popular holiday times, and at weekends or on Sundays only otherwise. The adult return fare from Llanfair to Castle was 35p and usually there were two or three return trips each day the railway operated. The time-table gave trains a generous allowance of 36 to 45 minutes for the 4¼ miles. This was a legacy of earlier days when track was bad. Also, so that late-comers may not be left behind after travelling a long distance to see the railway, each train is scheduled by the working time-table to leave the terminus a little later than the time made public. To say just how much later would destroy the object of the exercise! Anyway, the practice might be discontinued. When the line opens to Sylfaen it is intended to accelerate trains.

I attempt to render place names phonetically into English, though the results have an improbable look: Llanfair Caereinion— *Thlanvair Kareinion* (*ei* as *i* in *nine*); Cyfronydd—*Kuvronnuth* (*u* as in *cut*; *th* as in *the*); Sylfaen—*Sulvarn*.

The railway was built by the Welshpool and Llanfair Light Railway Company, opened in 1903 and worked by the Cambrian Railways Co. Both concerns were subsequently absorbed by the Great Western Railway, which put on a bus service from Welshpool to Dinas Mawddwy via Llanfair in 1925 and closed the Welshpool and Llanfair railway to passengers in 1931. Goods trains, however, continued into the 1950s by which time the line had become part of British Railways. It was the last public narrow-gauge railway in Britain to be operated commercially for general goods traffic—vindication for its promotors. Sufficient interest arose for passenger excursions to be arranged. Because the original coaches had been scrapped, passengers travelled in open wagons in which station seats had been fitted. And a very enjoyable day out it was.

After several false alarms the railway was closed in November 1956.

Following initial moves in Welshpool the previous August the Welshpool–Llanfair Railway Preservation Society was constituted at a meeting in London the same month as closure. Progress was slow, while it raised money and negotiated with British Railways and the Ministry of Transport. The first volunteer working parties found the line badly overgrown when they arrived in 1959, while the track, which BR had stated at the time of closure needed re-sleepering at a cost of £5,000, was deteriorating.

In January 1960 the Welshpool and Llanfair Light Railway Preservation Co. Ltd. was incorporated and took over from the society, which was dissolved. The company is limited by guarantee; first among its objects is 'to preserve, retain and restore the . . . railway extending from Welshpool to Llanfair Caereinion'. The big step forward came in October 1962 when the Minister of Transport made an order with the imposing if bureaucratic title: 'British Transport Commission (Welshpool and Llanfair) Light Railway (Leasing and Transfer) Order 1962'. This authorized the company to acquire, lease and operate the railway between Raven Square and Llanfair Caereinion.

The British Transport Commission—the overlord, at that period, of nationalized transport—granted the company a lease of the railway's land, track and buildings for twenty-one years from 25 December 1962. A handsome Christmas present! The rent was not high: for the first five years, £100 a year; for the second five years, £200 a year; and for the remainder of the term, £250 a year.

The section through Welshpool town was not included. Discussions with authorities had indicated that a light railway amendment order with road crossings in the town would not be granted. Before the town section was dismantled the company was able to use it for a few years for access by works trains to the standard-gauge station.

The railway was reopened for passenger trains from Llanfair to Castle Caereinion on 6 April 1963. Trains carried 9,934 passengers that year. For the 1964 season the service was extended to Sylfaen and 12,948 passengers were carried. On the night of Saturday 12 December 1964 came disaster.

Viewing the shallow, rocky, Afon Banwy from the train in summer it is difficult to realize that in winter it swells and floods extensively. On that December day, after a week of steady rain, it was already over its banks. Drizzle increased to a downpour and floods blocked roads to Welshpool. At 10.30 p.m. according to the account in *The Llanfair Railway Companion*, a party of volunteers ventured out to find the track at Dolrhyd Mill, near Llanfair, under two feet of rushing water; and at the Banwy viaduct water foamed against the piers as though each was the bows of a ship. As they returned to bed one morbidly imaginative member conjured up opening phrases from lurid accident reports.

Next morning the joke turned sour. The viaduct was very badly damaged. A pier had been undermined and shifted by the current, girder spans sagged on top of it.

Before the viaduct could be used again, the girders had to be jacked up, the old pier demolished and a new one built. The cost was quite beyond the company at that time. A flood damage appeal fund was set up, to which about 400 people contributed a total of £1,969. Part of the work was done by 16th Railway Regiment, Royal Engineers, as a training exercise, and part of it by the company's volunteers. To give access for army equipment the track had to be lifted from Heniarth Gate to the viaduct, and subsequently relaid.

During the first part of the following summer, a shuttle train service ran between Llanfair and Heniarth. Viaduct and track repairs were not completed until 13 August 1965, after which date the train service was resumed as far as Castle Caereinion only. Since 1965 traffic has grown steadily if not spectacularly to 43,313 passenger journeys in 1971.

The first steam locomotives to come to the preserved railway were the two handsome Beyer Peacock 0-6-0Ts which had worked it alone throughout its commercial existence. Both had been stored at Oswestry BR works after the line closed; No. 1 *The Earl* was generously purchased and presented by a member in 1961 and No. 2 *The Countess* cost the company £425 in 1962. Goods wagons and vans from the original stock were also obtained and are now used for works trains.

To reopen the line for passengers it was fortunately possible to obtain five bogie coaches of the correct gauge from the Admiralty's Chattenden and Upnor Railway in Kent. Four of these were toast-rack coaches, to two of which doors and windows are being fitted. The fifth is a comfortable modern saloon coach: according to a press report at the time, the company had to pay only £30 for this coach which had cost £3,000 to build four years earlier. Additional goods wagons came from the Chattenden railway, too.

In 1966 an anonymous member of the company purchased for it *Monarch*, the most powerful locomotive on Bowater's 2 ft. 6 in. gauge industrial light railway at Sittingbourne, Kent. *Monarch*, built only in 1953, is an up-to-date version of a Fairlie, with a single boiler and two driving bogies. She has not yet worked on the W & L—she is having a preserved railway long-term overhaul.

Four coaches arrived from Austria in 1968. With a shortage of suitable passenger rolling stock in the UK, it was fortunate for the W & L that one of its directors, Mr. F. S. Mayman, had business connections in Austria, where many 2 ft. 6 in. gauge railways still run. The coaches are typical of old Austrian narrow-gauge coaches—short and fat with balconies at the ends and slatted wooden seats inside. They were presented by the Zillertalbahn, a light railway in the Tyrol. Transport on standard-gauge rail wagons from Austria to Wales cost £880, of which £596 was defrayed by donations.

To join them a locomotive came from Austria in 1969. This is No. 10, an o–8–oT built in France in 1944 for German military railways—an origin comparable to that of the Festiniog Railway's *Mountaineer*, but a different war and a different side. Since the second world war she had been used on light railways in Austria. Her cost to the W & L was £650, which was increased to about £1,200 by transport. This was met by donations to an appeal fund. Import deposit of £414 was lent for six months by a W & L supporter. In service she has been found powerful and economical, able to burn slack coal discarded from the other locomotives. She has been named *Sir Drefaldwyn*, which is Welsh for Montgomeryshire.

The W & L has also on permanent loan a minuscule o–4–oT which once ran in a Glasgow gas-works and is now a museum piece, and has several diesels used on maintenance trains, and on passenger trains in emergency. In 1971 a group of members obtained the 1927 Kerr Stuart 0-6-2T *Joan* from the Antiguan Government sugar factory in the West Indies. After receiving a new boiler in 1950, she had been stored under cover since 1956 when diesels took over. Her cost to the W & L was £1,200 including transport. Since she was British built, no customs duty was payable.

Question: why does the preservation company need eight locomotives to run four or five miles of line when the old W & L managed with two for nine miles?

Answer: the old W & L was backed by the resources and maintenance facilities of a main-line railway company. The preservation company has to rely on its own resources—that is, those of members working in their spare time. It also has to provide for the future when the 40-year-old boilers of Nos. 1 and 2 wear out. And in any event the locomotives are an attraction to the public.

Locomotives and coaches appear in the liveries of their former owners. Of the two original locomotives, *The Earl* is in GWR green and *The Countess* in Cambrian Railways black. Chattenden and Upnor coaches are an exception: originally drab green, they are now red and cream. These colours stand out in the countryside and attract the attention of passers-by.

The Welshpool and Llanfair's traffic figures are modest compared with other Welsh lines, but it does have the edge over them in being near enough to England to cater in a big way for educational visits by schools. Parties of schoolchildren come from as far away as Birmingham and Liverpool. They travel on the train and *en route* it halts for half an hour for them to picnic in a riverside meadow. The railway arranges this beforehand with a farmer; its coaches have steps, so passengers are able to leave and join the train despite absence of a platform. The parties often continue to visit Powis Castle or the Shropshire Union Canal at Welshpool. In 1971, school parties brought 12,000 passenger-journeys to the W & L in five weeks.

Special trains run for photographers, with more than one photographic run-past. That is to say the train stops, drops passengers and sets back down the line. It comes storming past them, throwing out clouds of smoke and steam, then stops and sets back to pick them up.

Most ordinary passengers are people out for the day from the

West Midlands or North-west, with a sprinkling from all parts of
the country. The level of traffic remains even throughout the week.
People on their way to or from a holiday in Wales often break the
journey with a trip on the W & L. There is no local traffic, though
some might develop when the train service reaches Welshpool
again. Ironically, just at the time when the railway is working
towards this, there is talk of withdrawing the bus service between
the two towns.

The course of events is sometimes strange. In 1931 it would have
needed a good crystal ball to foresee that development.

In its first season, 1963, the preserved railway's income from
running trains covered operating costs—coal, oil, etc.—but left
little over for maintenance. In 1964 the annual membership
subscription was raised from £1 11s. od. to £2 2s. od. In these
delicate circumstances the Banwy did more damage than could be
seen on the viaduct. In 1965, when for half the season trains were
able to run only between Llanfair and Heniarth, traffic income was
only £759, but the cost of operating the railway was £2,955. Even
allowing for income from subscriptions and donations, and profit
on sales, there was a net loss for the year of £608. Since then things
have slowly improved. In 1966 there was a net surplus of £141
for the year, and in 1968 the overall deficit was eliminated, but in
1970 the cost of operating the railway—£4,250—was still greater
than traffic receipts—£3,605. That there was a net surplus of
£930 for the year was due in the main to income from sales and
subscriptions.

The Banwy disaster did have one good effect; it resulted, in
1965, in a record total of members—over 1,100. Since then membership has varied between 850 and 980; members get free travel on
trains. There are eight area groups. Notable are area organizations
as close to the railway as Shrewsbury and Oswestry.

The railway has minimal paid staff, only the general manager
and, in summer, two ladies who serve in the tea bar and shop at
Llanfair. Advertisements in 1971 for a general manager attracted
80 applicants. Volunteer members do all tasks necessary to maintain and run the railway, including locomotive driver and signalman. For flexibility, those trained for one job often learn others
as well. Twelve to fifteen per cent of total membership work on
the railway on a regular basis.

Things do not always run smoothly. In August 1970, recorded
Llanfair Railway Journal, seven members took a platelayer's
petrol trolley from Llanfair yard and went for a joy-ride down the
line with neither permission nor train staff. For this they were
sent away the next morning. Such things are neither exclusive to
the W & L nor, on the whole, common.

The railway's administration is divided into four departments
under the general manager: mechanical, itself divided into locomotive, and carriage and wagon; civil engineering, which includes
signals and telegraphs; traffic, that is guards, signalmen etc.; and
shop and tea bar.

The railway is operated by train staff and ticket system. The
only loop between Llanfair and Castle Caereinion is at Cyfronydd.
Passenger trains do not cross there regularly but it is used for
special passenger or works trains to cross scheduled passenger
trains. To unlock point levers, an old train staff now reduced in
status to a points key is issued to guards by Llanfair signalman.
This official is in effect controller and is in charge of train staff
working.

The signal box and GWR-style signals at Llanfair were a
development by the preservation company. Although the Department of the Environment does not yet require the station to be
signalled, it has inspected and approved the installation. Certainly
it is valuable, when as many as four locomotives may be moving
within the station at once, to have all movements under control of
one signalman.

An omnibus telephone line links all stations and is used to
describe trains and request permission for them to proceed. There
is a second, local, circuit round station and yard at Llanfair.

At present trains have no continuous brakes. In preparation for
working down Golfa incline to Welshpool, locomotives and
coaches are gradually being equipped with vacuum brakes. The
Austrian coaches arrived vacuum-fitted, but unfortunately their
brakes do not fail safe, so modifications are needed.

When the Welshpool town section of the line was denied to the
preservation company it was cut off from the locomotive shed
which was at the far terminus. It had to base itself at Llanfair and
make the best of it. A workshop was set up in the goods shed and
recently a two-road locomotive shed has been built, partly by

contract, partly by volunteers. Coaches still stand in the open.

Much of the track, which comprises original flat-bottom rail spiked to second-hand BR sleepers cut in half, has been relaid by members. Maintenance is being mechanized. As soon as work is complete to Sylfaen, it is intended to start on the Sylfaen to Welshpool section.

In the distant future, the company hopes to own the railway.

5   The Bluebell Railway

Between those who live north of London and those who live to the south lies a gulf. Attitudes of mind are quite at variance. Southerners, I suspect, consider that civilization ends somewhere about Regents Park. As for me, I live north of London and am well aware that, to the south, there is nothing but houses and cars until you reach the sea.

This impression is justified, I submit, by observation, particularly when travelling south on a main road, or, to a lesser extent, in a main-line railway train. However, there is another South, off the beaten track, and it is always pleasant to rediscover how delightful it really is. In the Sussex Weald there is a countryside of low undulating hills, small fields, pasture and plough, sleepy brooks and frequent little woods. The whole is tinged golden, with luck, by autumn sun.

Through this landscape puff the Bluebell Railway trains. From them it is seen at its best.

The railway is one of the last surviving sections of the series of wayward branch lines which served these parts. Some clue to their disappearance is found in the location of its stations. The station at one end of the line, Horsted Keynes, is set in the woods a long mile from the village of that name. The station at the other end, Sheffield Park, is close to no village at all.

In 1960, the Bluebell Railway was the first closed branch line of British Railways to be reopened privately as a preserved railway. It was also a pioneer standard-gauge preserved railway. It is now isolated from the main railway system and 5 miles long, with an intermediate halt at Freshfield, 2¼ miles from Sheffield Park. Most of the way to Horsted Keynes is uphill, though there is a downhill stretch past Freshfield. The ruling gradient is 1 in 75.

Bluebell policy is to 'preserve the puffer for posterity', alive on a rural branch line. Deliberate intent to recreate the appearance of times past is notable. Locomotives and coaches (most of which originated on railways in the South of England) are restored to old liveries; staff wear old-fashioned uniform, Victorian costume appears often, and stations are embellished with ancient but colourful enamel posters.

Sheffield Park station is being restored to the appearance of a station of the London, Brighton and South Coast Railway, of which company's system the line which is now the Bluebell Railway formed part before the 1923 grouping. Signals are original LBSC items collected and re-installed at this station, original paraffin lamp fittings remain and the station is painted in the LBSC colours of purple-brown and stone. Horsted Keynes, on the other hand, is to be kept like a station of the Southern Railway—to which company the railway belonged after the grouping. It has electric light, green paint, Southern Railway signals. But some LBSC signals are among them, for such were still familiar in SR days.

Headquarters of the railway are at Sheffield Park, on main road A275 between East Grinstead and Lewes and some 40 miles from London. Here are buffet, bookstall and a museum of small exhibits. By public road transport in 1971 the station was inaccessible—the bus service past it was too limited to be of use to visitors to the railway. Many motor-coach companies run excursions to the Bluebell Railway. They come from the London area, and from seaside towns from Margate in the east to Portsmouth in the west. A surprising exception in 1971, despite efforts by the railway to interest coach operators, was Brighton, one of the nearest resorts.

Horsted Keynes is served by Southdown buses from East Grinstead and Haywards Heath. The nearest stop is a quarter of a mile from the station. By car, several by-roads lead to it, and my personal preference is to visit the Bluebell Railway via Horsted Keynes. That there is more to see at Sheffield Park simply gives a purpose to the train journey; while Horsted Keynes, a big station, still under-used (it was formerly a junction with four tracks and five platforms) seems to me a more authentic introduction to the railway than Sheffield Park, a small country station thrust into the limelight and sometimes rather crowded.

At Horstead Keynes, too, as you wait for the train its arrival is heralded by all the right puffing noises as it makes its way up

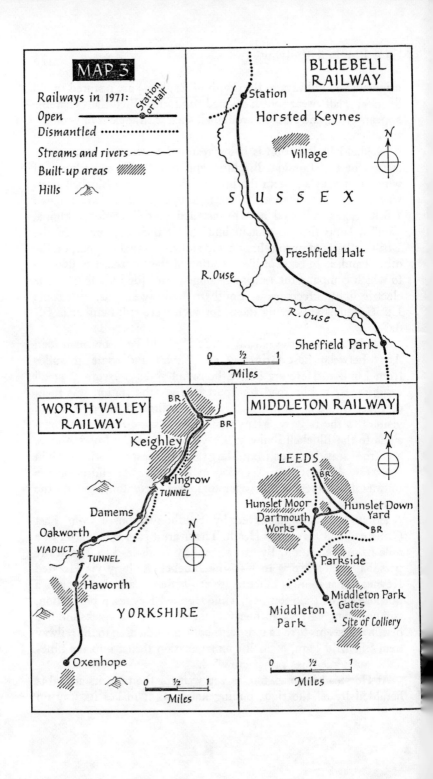

MAP 3

Railways in 1971:
Open
Dismantled
Streams and rivers
Built-up areas
Hills

Station or Halt

BLUEBELL RAILWAY

Station
Horsted Keynes

Village

S U S S E X

N

Freshfield Halt

R. Ouse

R. Ouse

Sheffield Park

0   ½   1
Miles

WORTH VALLEY RAILWAY

BR
BR
Keighley

Ingrow
TUNNEL

Damems

Oakworth
VIADUCT   TUNNEL

Haworth

YORKSHIRE

N

Oxenhope

0   ½   1
Miles

MIDDLETON RAILWAY

N

LEEDS

BR

Hunslet Moor
Dartmouth
Works

Hunslet Down
Yard

BR

Parkside

Middleton Park
Gates

Middleton
Park

Site of Colliery

0   ½   1
Miles

7 *upper* Imported engine. *Mountaineer* heads a Festiniog Railway train between Tan-y-bwlch and Dduallt. (N. F. Gurley.) *lower The Railway Children's* train. L & Y Rly, o–6–o (with fictitiously lettered tender) takes a train up the Worth Valley Railway for the film makers. (J. A. Cox.)

8 Industry. *Upper:* Middleton Railway visitors' train with Sentinel locomotive stands at Hunslet Moor. (Author.)
lower Foxfield Light Railway saddle-tank locomotive *J. T. Daly* approaches train at Blythe Bridge. (Author.)

through the steep, damp slippery cuttings which lead to the station. At Sheffield Park trains off the down gradient drift into the station so that you hardly notice.

Trains run all year round on the Bluebell Railway. Its passengers comprise not only holiday-makers from the south coast, but also weekend visitors to the locality and people out for the day from their homes, both nearby and in London. The peak season, though, is from about 20 July until the end of September. Residents near Freshfield Halt sometimes take the train to catch a bus from Horsted Keynes, and perhaps twice a year someone travels who actually needs to get from one end to the other.

The journey of 15 minutes cost 30p in 1971. There is a train service every day from June to September and at Easter; at weekends and on Wednesdays in spring and autumn; at weekends in November and February; and on Sundays and Boxing Day in December and January. The number of return journeys daily ranges from eleven down to two.

On Boxing Day 1970, when severe weather brought chaos to BR electric services in the South, Bluebell trains were steaming confidently through nine inches of snow, complete with Father Christmas and carol singers. In 1971, milder Christmas weather brought some 2,250 visitors in three days, which meant nine-coach trains. Intending winter passengers will be relieved to learn that according to the working time-table trains must be steam-heated from October to April.

The Bluebell Railway is part of the line built by the Lewes and East Grinstead Railway Co. to link the towns of its name. It was opened in 1882. A year later a branch was added from Horsted Keynes to the main London-Brighton line near Haywards Heath. The Lewes and East Grinstead company had the backing of the London, Brighton and South Coast Railway: before long the latter company took over completely.

For the next 72 years the Lewes to East Grinstead line served its region adequately if unspectacularly. It came to be regarded with affection by passengers, and from the abundance of flowers along its course the section south of Horsted Keynes acquired the nickname *Bluebell Line*. North of Horsted Keynes it was the *Primrose Line*, and there was a *Cuckoo Line* nearby. The Bluebell Line became, in 1948, part of the Southern Region of British

Railways; and, in 1955, suffering from an excess of road competition, it was closed.

Not without opposition. Opposition in the person of a local lady established that the Act of Parliament which had transferred the line from the Lewes and East Grinstead company to the London, Brighton and South Coast required the latter to run a daily minimum service of four trains each way. As successor to the LBSC, British Railways inherited the obligation: they had to reopen the line, and did so in August 1956.

Unfortunately it did not last long. In March 1958 British Railways were able to withdraw the train service the second time. But controversy continued. A year later, in March 1959, three students, again following Talyllyn and Festiniog examples, called a public meeting at Haywards Heath. Here the Lewes and East Grinstead Railway Preservation Society was formed and a committee elected. The committee appointed trustees of the society to negotiate with British Railways.

To the trustees, to preserve the whole line was impracticable, but to preserve part of it was possible, and the Sheffield Park to Horstead Keynes section most possible, for only these two stations had a water supply for locomotives. That at Horsted Keynes, however, was adequate only for emergencies, and in any event the station was still in use by BR as the terminus of the branch from Haywards Heath which had been electrified between the wars. The first approach to British Railways for a lease with option to purchase met with ridicule—modified to an offer to sell the railway from Sheffield Park to a point just south of Horsted Keynes for £55,000 to be raised in three months; and while the society was doing so it could rent the booking hall at Sheffield Park station for five shillings a week!

The trustees jumped at the opportunity offered by the five shillings a week. The society reconstituted itself as the Bluebell Railway Preservation Society, with aims to preserve all or part of the Bluebell Line and to preserve on it historic locomotives, rolling stock and other items of railway interest, and by negotiation the trustees obtained reduction of the asking price to £34,000. Even this was more than the society could afford and negotiations continued to obtain a lease. To satisfy BR the trustees found backers prepared to guarantee up to £10,000 in event of liquidation. Then

BR intimated that they would offer a lease—and recommend the Ministry of Transport to grant a light railway order—only to a company rather than to individuals.

So the trustees formed The Bluebell Railway Ltd. Its directors were, and are, the society's trustees. Should a director cease to be a trustee, he is disqualified from continuing in his post. Objects of the company were to purchase, lease or otherwise acquire all or any of the railway from East Grinstead to Lewes and carry on the business of running it. (As is usual with companies, there are many other objects included in the memorandum of association. In the Bluebell's instance they range from being carriers of passengers and goods by land, water or air to being refreshment contractors, restaurant keepers, sugar and sweetmeat merchants, farmers and dairymen!) Original trustee/directors included Horace May, later well known as the railway's general manager, and Captain Peter Manisty, subsequently chairman of the A.R.P.S. Of the company's nominal capital of £100 in £1 shares, the 1970 balance sheet shows only eight shares to have been issued. These have been allotted to trustees to qualify as directors. There are no shareholders other than the trustees and no dividend is paid. The Bluebell society is run by a committee with up to 14 members, comprising trustees and others.

This society/trustee/company set-up worked well for ten years. Regrettably, however, it has not been proof against internal disagreement which arose in the Bluebell society as in others which embrace all types and temperaments. In the winter of 1970–71 conflict became so serious that three members went to the extreme of applying to a High Court judge to ban a general meeting of the society of which insufficient notice had been given; and the judge agreed. At the society's subsequent annual general meeting in March three additional shareholder/directors were appointed to the company for a year, and friendly co-operation now appears to have replaced differences of opinion. With the benefit of hindsight, however, it seems to me that the Bluebell society would have done better if it had done as the Welshpool & Llanfair society did in 1960 and formed itself into a company limited by guarantee.

At any rate the first directors were eventually able to negotiate an acceptable deal with BR: a five-year lease with option to purchase. The rent was £2,250 a year. BR would not allow Bluebell

trains into Horsted Keynes station—to enter it they would have
had to cross tracks used by BR trains to reach the goods yard. The
Bluebell Railway had to build its own terminus, a platform made
from sleepers, and called Bluebell Halt, where the line crossed a
road short of the station. British Railways applied for an L.R.O.
for the section Sheffield Park to Bluebell Halt, and when it was
granted, for a transfer order in favour of Bluebell Railway Ltd.
The line was inspected by Ministry of Transport inspecting
officer and passed: the transfer order was made on 27 June 1960.

In the meantime the society had been looking for locomotives
and rolling stock. In those days steam locomotives, though on their
way out, were still commonplace. The locomotive the society
obtained was both appropriate and historically interesting: an
o–6–oT built by the LBSCR in 1875 of the class called Terriers.
Fifty of them were built for suburban trains but later became
familiar on branch lines and light railways. The Bluebell's example
reverted to its original number and name—55 *Stepney*. She was
purchased from British Railways with two coaches—a third-class
non-corridor coach which had originated on the London and South
Western Railway in 1900 and a corridor first-class/third-class/
guard/luggage composite coach from the Southern Railway of the
twenties. Price for the three was £750.

Cost of installing a loop for the locomotive to run round its
train at Bluebell Halt was prohibitive. Instead, since the driver of
a passenger train must normally be at the front, the Bluebell
decided to run with a locomotive at each end. They approached
BR for another Terrier. It is astonishing to reflect that as recently
as 1960 BR's response was that for a few years they would need all
such locomotives they possessed. Instead they provided another
locomotive of similar size—a South Eastern and Chatham Railway
P class o–6–oT built in 1909.

The railway was reopened on 7 August 1960, a day of blazing
sunshine. Members turned out in Victorian costume, crowds
jammed the platforms, film cameramen balanced themselves on
roofs, and the Temperance Seven band syncopated away in the
background. *The Times* reported attendance of over 2,000.

To complete the story of the Bluebell Line's change of ownership: as the end of the five-year lease approached, not only did the
Bluebell society not wish to continue with short leases, which

inhibited capital expenditure on much-needed developments, but British Railways, after a change of policy, would consider only sale rather than lease of unwanted property. By then they were no longer using Horsted Keynes station, as the branch to Haywards Heath was closed: they asked £65,000 for the Bluebell Line from Sheffield Park to Horsted Keynes inclusive. The Bluebell Society, having started a line-purchase fund, had £20,000 available. While negotiations proceeded the lease was extended, until late in 1967 a figure of £43,500 was agreed.

At the crucial moment the Bluebell's intention to raise the balance of the purchase price by bank loan was defeated by government imposition of a credit squeeze. There was a real danger that the line would close.

Fortunately after still further negotiations it was agreed with BR that £20,000 should be paid on completion of the purchase— eventually achieved on 18 October 1968—and the balance by quarterly instalments, with interest, over five years until 1973. As security the line was mortgaged to the British Railways Board.

Included in the purchase were ten cottages, six of which were subsequently auctioned, for £7,150. With the proceeds and with other funds, mostly from income, the company succeeded in paying off the mortgage in 1971, more than two years early. For the first time in its twelve-year history, the Bluebell Railway Preservation Society was free from the invisible but substantial burden of paying for its railway.

In 1960 trains carried 15,000 passengers, running at weekends only until the end of October, when the railway closed for the winter. During the summer of 1961, 92,100 passengers were carried and weekday trains ran for a short period. In 1962 and 1963, after Horsted Keynes goods yard had been closed, Bluebell trains were permitted to use one track in Horsted Keynes passenger station which they could reach without crossing any tracks used by BR trains from Haywards Heath. The Bluebell trains had to carry a British Railways pilotman, at the Bluebell Railway's expense, and still had to run with an engine at each end because no run-round loop was accessible. A halt was opened in 1962 at Holywell, where the railway crossed the road from Horsted Keynes to Lindfield. It was closed after two summers at the request of the local authority because of road congestion caused by parked cars attracted to it.

Several through special trains came from British Railways to Sheffield Park. Often they were hauled by historic steam locomotives, sometimes Bluebell locomotives went on to BR as far as Victoria and Brighton to fetch them. All this came to an end in October 1963 when the Haywards Heath branch was closed. Most of it has since been dismantled; a Bluebell locomotive (usually No. 2650, a North London Railway o-6-oT) was hired to contractors for the melancholy task of powering demolition trains first on the branch and then from Horsted Keynes north to East Grinstead. However, as soon as BR closed Horsted Keynes, the Bluebell Railway rented it; and when demolition trains through the station ceased, altered the signalling so that in 1965 a run-round loop was at last available and only one engine was needed for each train. In 1970, 254,000 passengers made journeys on the Bluebell Railway.

To join the first two locomotives have come many others, to a total of 18. There are now two Terriers—the second to arrive, *Fenchurch*, was not only the first of the class to be built in 1872 but is now the oldest standard-gauge locomotive in service on a preserved railway—and there are three SECR P class o-6-oTs, one of which is painted a Bluebell Railway blue livery complete with coat of arms and motto *Floreat vapor*. To operate several locomotives of the same class eases maintenance for parts are interchangeable, though it displeases enthusiasts for history who prefer to see locomotives of different classes preserved. They are perhaps appeased by other early arrivals: LBSC o-6-2T No. 473 *Birch Grove*, LSWR 4-4-2T No. 488 and the NLR o-6-oT. As on the Welsh lines all these locomotives belong to the operating company.

In 1962 came Great Western 4-4-o No. 3217 *Earl of Berkeley*. This locomotive had been purchased privately when withdrawn by BR and was loaned to the Bluebell—the first instance, I believe, of an arrangement which has since become commonplace on preserved railways. Locomotives of its class had been built in the thirties from parts of much older locomotives of the Duke and Bulldog classes: hence they gained the clumsy nickname *Dukedog*. In 1971, No. 3217's tender was found to have a badly corroded

underframe. Pending repairs, the tender from SECR C class
0–6–0 No. 592 was attached to it, and the locomotive promptly
became known as the *Seadog*. . . . The class C locomotive had
arrived on the Bluebell Railway only in 1970, having been bought
by the Wainwright 'C' Preservation Society some years previously.
It was awaiting repairs.

In 1969 an anonymous member purchased and donated British
Railways standard class four 4–6–0 No. 75027, built only in 1954.
Its reign as the biggest engine on the line was eclipsed in 1971
when SR West Country class 4–6–2 *Blackmore Vale* arrived. She
was preserved by the Bulleid Pacific Preservation Society and
along with its other possessions was moved to the Bluebell Railway
from the Longmoor Military Railway when the attempt to set up a
steam railway there failed. For the same reason the Southern
Locomotive Preservation Co. Ltd.'s SR USA class 0–6–0T and
coaches were moved from Longmoor to Sheffield Park.

Locomotive No. 24 is an 0–6–0 saddle tank of, unusually for the
Bluebell, industrial railway origin. It was purchased in 1969 from
Stewarts and Lloyds Minerals Ltd. and the cost, including transport from Rutland, was £500, raised by members of the railway's
locomotive department. After overhaul it is intended to use it for
shunting at Sheffield Park. Three other small industrial locomotives are now exhibits rather than pieces of motive power.

The stock of coaches has expanded to include several more
SECR and Southern Railway coaches, and two built to SR designs
by British Railways in 1949 and 1950. Made obsolete by electrification to Bournemouth, they were purchased by the Bluebell in
1970 and repainted in SR green livery by British Railways before
delivery. Other coaches include an observation car which once
saw service on the London and North Western Railway's Conway
Valley line in Wales and four Metropolitan Railway coaches which
previously ran on the Chesham branch. Goods vehicles are few:
they include several vans used as headquarters by the signals and
telegraphs and other departments, and as stores.

The Metropolitan coaches had the misfortune to become the
visible evidence of the consequences of the hidden struggle over
lease and purchase of the line. When The Bluebell Railway Ltd.
took it over there was no covered accommodation for rolling stock,
and, while the line was on short lease, expenditure on a carriage

shed could not be justified. Not until purchase of the line was complete could it be considered, and even then there was the mortgage to be repaid. Meanwhile the coaches stood outside in all weathers—paint peeled, woodwork decayed. This was all too obvious to visitors: unfortunately the reasons were not.

In 1970 an appeal for a carriage shed was launched: 'Save our rotting stock!' It raised some £5,000. With this, and the balance found by the company, a steel and corrugated asbestos shed was built at Horsted Keynes by contract for £7,859. It covers three sidings in the goods yard which were already suitably aligned; a fourth is being installed by society members. No half-measures about this shed—when track is complete it will hold 14 coaches.

Locomotives in 1971 did not fare so well. A £10,000 appeal has been launched for a new shed which will include a workshop. A small concrete shed was built for the reopening; it has been temporarily extended with scaffolding, and a small workshop built alongside. Here running maintenance and minor overhauls are done. In 1971 locomotive No. 488 was dispatched to the Swindon works of British Rail Engineering Ltd. for general overhaul, estimated to cost £12,000.

The Bluebell Railway's staff numbered five in 1971: general manager, three men on locomotive maintenance and driving, and a permanent way ganger who used to hold the same position on the line with BR. About 100 members of the society, out of a total of about 1,250, work regularly on the railway as volunteers. Most of them live within 60 miles of it. Departments include locomotive, carriage and wagon, guards, signals and telegraphs and carriage cleaning. Catering, in station buffets, is by contract.

In 1971 the railway was still operated by train staff, without tickets. For flexibility, electric train staff equipment was being installed, using original LBSCR instruments. Horsted Keynes signal box, with 40 levers (although not all are in use), is the largest on a preserved railway. An underground cable has replaced the overhead telephone line between Sheffield Park and Horsted Keynes as wire was stolen and poles had rotted.

Restoration and development of the Bluebell Railway have been paid for by subscriptions, railway revenue, and loans and donations from well-wishers. The railway has received no big grants from public bodies, nor has it raised money by issuing shares or loan stock. It has found a useful source of revenue in providing facilities for films to be made for showing in cinemas and on television—this amounted to £1,511 in 1970. It has also been seen as the background in many advertisements.

The Bluebell Railway Ltd.'s accounts show that running expenses in 1970 were £23,881, of which the largest item was £8,274 for wages and national insurance; total railway income was £29,522, of which £24,701 was derived from fares and car parks. A Tenth Anniversary appeal, for the carriage shed, raised £4,596 during the year: this and a donation from the BRPS brought the surplus up to £12,016. Much of it was used in mortgage repayments and carriage-shed construction. The future seems promising.

6   The Middleton Railway

The Middleton Railway looks like a scruffy industrial siding in a scruffy part of Leeds. There is absolutely nothing to show how remarkable it is.

Regrettably, National Trust notices are not exhibited where it impinges on the highway. The National Trust protects the railway but its policy reserves such notices for property which it actually owns.

The Middleton Railway makes many claims to fame:

It is the only preserved railway which operates principally for freight traffic.

It was the first standard-gauge preserved railway. (This claim results from a demonstration passenger service which ran in June 1960 on the basis: 'travel free, at your own risk, and make a donation to Leeds University Rag Week funds'. Regular goods trains did not start until 1 September, by which time the Bluebell Railway was already running scheduled passenger trains. So honours seem about even.)

As long ago as 1812, Middleton operated the first steam railway locomotives in regular commercial service.

Earlier still, in 1758, it was the first railway authorized (but not incorporated) by Act of Parliament.

It is, it claims quite simply, the oldest surviving railway in the world.

So old is the Middleton Railway, that when the Talyllyn Railway was new the Middleton was already as old as the Talyllyn is today.

In addition to freight trains the Middleton Railway Trust runs steam trains for visitors. They operate between Hunslet Moor and Middleton Park Gates, on the afternoons of Saturdays, Sundays and bank holidays from March to October, starting at 14.00 and continuing at half-hourly intervals until about 16.30. The journey takes 10 minutes each way and cost 10p adult return in 1971. Sometimes special trains penetrate other parts of the railway.

Hunslet Moor Halt is adjacent to Moor Road on the south side of Leeds. It is on bus routes 74 and 76 from Park Row, opposite Leeds City station. It is also close to an intersection on the M1 motorway extension which was being built in 1971. Hunslet Moor is not wild open country—it is no more rural than the commons that survive in London suburbs at, for instance, Clapham and Ealing.

The halt is a platform beside a spur of track which once extended further into the centre of Leeds. The visitors' train usually comprises an LMS guard's brake-van and an open wagon in either of which people ride. Books and badges are sold in the van. Locomotives are small, often of industrial railway origin. The train engine remains at the Leeds end to propel it up gradients as steep as 1 in 27 to Middleton Park Gates Halt, a mile to the south.

Immediately on leaving Hunslet Moor a branch trails in from the east. This is the Balm Road branch which connects with British Railways at Hunslet Down goods yard, a third of a mile away. The Middleton main line pierces the M1 embankment by a short and brand-new tunnel. Beyond it another branch trails in, this time from the west; it comes from Dartmouth Works and other private sidings. Between these sidings and the BR connection run the Middleton Railway's freight trains and at Dartmouth Works is its depot which is open to visitors by prior arrangement only.

At the time of my 1971 visit the passenger train was running to Dartmouth Works. Junction and branch had been re-aligned for the M1 (their original alignment would have necessitated two tunnels) and for this the main line had been broken and not then re-connected beyond the junction. But beyond the break it continued uphill beneath Parkside bridge which formerly carried the BR branch, now closed, from Beeston Junction to Hunslet East. Beyond it, to the east, was an area where colliery waste tips were being levelled out; to the west are fields. Curving across them could be seen the track-bed of the Middleton Light Railway. This was part of Leeds' electric tramway system. It was completed in 1949, under an L.R.O. made as recently as 1946; in 1959 the whole lot was closed.

The Middleton Railway proper terminates by an entrance to wooded Middleton Park, though until recently it continued into Middleton Colliery (Broom Pit), now a flat and vacant site, black with coal dust. The Middleton Railway's surroundings are dreary but will probably improve with redevelopment. There is a possibility that the Commonwealth Games complex will be developed nearby.

The Middleton trust had great hopes of establishing a museum and covered depot—which it lacks—in the old colliery buildings. It underestimated the destructive energy of local vandals. When the National Coal Board vacated the colliery in 1970, windows were bricked up and doors reinforced. Within three months the buildings had been so badly damaged that they were unsafe and had to be demolished.

It is difficult to credit this until you have visited the area and seen, as I did, a modern factory, left vacant for only a short time, with every window smashed. Vandalism and theft are big problems to the railway. In 1966, 190 ft. of track was stolen: chairs were smashed by sledge-hammers and rails cut by oxy-acetylene. Fortunately the section was not in daily use. Throughout the railway spring steel keys have to be used to wedge rails in chairs. Wood keys common elsewhere were regarded here by local inhabitants as a free issue of firewood by a benevolent railway.

It is a shame that the railway was unable to establish its museum at the colliery, although it now has other plans, for it was the colliery that first caused construction of the railway.

Records of coal mining at Middleton go back to 1646. By the 1750s mines belonged to the Brandling family; in order to sell coal competitively in Leeds Charles Brandling decided to construct a wagonway. He made agreements with owners of land needed and had these ratified by Act of Parliament on 9 June 1758. The wagonway he built probably had wooden rails, like other wagonways of the period, later replaced by iron rails. The wagons themselves were pulled by horses.

During the Napoleonic wars, high cost of horses and fodder caused John Blenkinsop, manager at Middleton, to seek alternatives. Experiments had previously been made elsewhere with steam locomotives: those which Blenkinsop now had built, in Leeds by Matthew Murray, were the first to be put into regular service, on

12 August 1812. This was two years before George Stephenson's first locomotive. (Stephenson visited the line in 1813.)

The Middleton engines attracted much attention, both in Britain and abroad, and ran successfully until 1835. By that time profits were going down, the Brandling estates were in the hands of trustees, Blenkinsop was dead and fodder was cheap. Horses returned.

In 1862 the Brandling estates, including the wagonway, were sold. The purchaser formed the Middleton Estate and Colliery Co. Steam locomotives were re-introduced in 1866, and in 1875 a diversion three-quarters of a mile long was built to avoid a rope-worked incline on the original route, the site of which is now Old Run Road. The main line described above is on this diversion, except for a few hundred yards at its southern end; the northern end of the diversion rejoined the original route near the modern Hunslet Moor Halt.

In 1881 the track, previously 4 ft. 1 in. gauge, was widened to standard-gauge. About this time the line was linked to the main railway system by a siding at its northern end. The Balm Road branch and connection were completed in 1895. In 1899 the Great Northern Railway opened its Beeston–Hunslet branch; this too was connected to the Middleton Railway, at Parkside Junction.

Links with main-line railways enabled goods traffic to be interchanged, which encouraged construction of private sidings. Those which today serve the Dartmouth Works of Clayton, Son & Co. Ltd. and metal merchants Robinson & Birdsell adjoining, were constructed in 1920.

In the 1940s, the Middleton Estate and Colliery Co., anticipating nationalization of the coal-mining industry, split its interests. The new Middleton Fireclay Company controlled the estates, and the railway. After nationalization the National Coal Board operated trains over the private company's track. Until 1947 the railway continued its historic function of carrying coal from Middleton to Leeds, but in that year traffic was discontinued north of Moor Depot, itself about a quarter of a mile north of Hunslet Moor Halt.

In 1958, because of the cost of track renewals, the National Coal Board proposed to discontinue using the railway and to build a road into the colliery. Such a road would have led to heavy traffic through a residential area nearby: it was opposed by Leeds City Council.

The same year, to celebrate the railway's bicentenary, an excursion was arranged over it jointly by the Railway and Canal Historical Society and the Railway Correspondence and Travel Society. Intrepid passengers rode in open wagons. The problem of access to the colliery was resolved by re-laying the half-mile section of the Middleton Railway from Parkside Junction into the colliery for use by British Railways locomotives and trains. This was done in 1959, and the rest of the railway was closed.

In September 1959 members of the Leeds University Union Railway Society had the idea of acquiring a short stretch of line to display railway museum pieces. The Middleton was the obvious choice. On the other hand, the union consultative panel, not surprisingly, did not approve of a union society running a railway. In December members of the railway society voted unanimously to found the Middleton Railway Preservation Society. Chairman of the meeting was Dr. R. F. Youell, staff president of the university railway society, whose name was to become as closely linked with the Middleton Railway as that of Brandling or Blenkinsop.

The preservation society converted itself into the Middleton Railway Trust in 1962 and subsequently became a registered charity. It had four trustees as legal custodians of its property. In 1971 the trust was planning to form itself into a company limited by guarantee. It was negotiating with the Charity Commissioners to remain a charity and intended to retain its name without alteration.

When formed, the preservation society did not envisage regular operation of the railway. It staged a ceremonial reopening, using a train comprised of an 0-6-0 diesel locomotive and one coach. Both were interesting vehicles: the locomotive, built by the Hunslet Engine Co. in 1932, was the first diesel locomotive to be operated on a British main line railway (the LMS). Repurchased by its maker, it was loaned and later sold to the Middleton trust, which named it *John Alcock* after Hunslet's chairman. The coach was a large double-deck tramcar from the then recently closed Swansea and Mumbles Railway. Trains carried 7,700 passengers.

From these demonstration runs arose the idea of operating the line for freight: several firms with private sidings had been left without a rail service since the line closed.

One of them, Clayton, Son & Co. Ltd., had bought the bulk of the line north of Parkside from liquidators of the Middleton Fireclay Co. and Clayton gave operation of the railway to the Middleton R.P.S. In view of the outstanding historic importance of the railway, Clayton also entered into a protective covenant with the National Trust. This provides that the railway will not be removed or disturbed. Today, the Middleton Railway Trust is the National Trust's agent for operating and maintaining this part of the railway.

In 1968 Middleton Colliery closed. This gave the Middleton trust the opportunity to acquire the section of line south of Parkside. Following its usual procedure the National Coal Board offered the land to Leeds Corporation, which purchased it; and then leased the land under this southern section of the railway to the Middleton trust. The railway track itself was purchased by the trust, after a public appeal for funds, for £1,450; it was handed over in February 1970. Prior to this, in July 1969, brake-van passenger trains had started to run over it by permission of the N.C.B.

The Middleton Railway Trust offers a daily freight service. Traffic has varied as follows:

1961	12,468 tons	1966	5,700 tons
1962	6,764 ,,	1967	4,480 ,,
1963	6,624 ,,	1968	3,661 ,,
1964	8,822 ,,	1969	1,667 ,,
1965	9,781 ,,	1970	5,854 ,,
		1971	5,600 tons approx.

Principal traffic at the time of writing is wagons of processed scrap-metal dispatched by Robinson & Birdsell to steelworks at Sheffield. Clayton build large process plant—that is, gas holders, oil refinery equipment, etc. They need to receive steel plate and dispatch finished products. Unfortunately, since 1968 little of this traffic has passed over the Middleton Railway, the innocent victim of a difference of opinion between Clayton and British Rail over demurrage. At present BR road lorries deliver the bulk of the steel plate from a goods depot three miles away. There are hopes that the traffic may return to the Middleton Railway.

The number of trains varies according to traffic offering. Usually

there is one return trip every weekday. In May 1971 traffic was
running at about ten 16-ton wagons a week. The railway is busiest
in winter—August is a slack month. All freight traffic passes to or
from British Rail and is carried in BR wagons. So far as BR is
concerned, the Middleton Railway is treated as a private siding.
No through freight rates are offered and customers get separate
bills from BR and the Middleton Railway.

None of the locomotives used on the Middleton Railway prior
to 1959 survives there. All locomotives now present have been
acquired by the Middleton trust (or, before 1962, preservation
society), and most are its property. Some have been bought, some
presented by former owners. Steam locomotives include 0-4-0
saddle tank *Matthew Murray*, built by Bagnall as recently as 1943
and so small that its cab is scarcely taller than an open wagon, and
larger 0-4-0 saddle tank *Henry de Lacy II* which burned oil when
acquired in 1968 but has now been converted to burn coal like the
other locomotives. No. 54 is a 'Sentinel' locomotive, with the high
steam pressure of 275 lb. per sq. in. and wheels driven by chains
instead of rods. No. 1310 is an inside-cylindered 0-4-0T restored
to the livery of its former owner, the North Eastern Railway; it
now belongs to Steam Power Trust '65.

Several diesel locomotives supplement *John Alcock*. Usually
goods trains are hauled by diesels and passenger trains by steam
locomotives, but the opposite sometimes occurs.

A steam crane (at least 92 years old) is frequently used to
re-lay track, and a Midland Railway hand crane often assists.
Goods rolling stock includes a genuine Middleton Estate and
Colliery Co. wagon of about 1890, repurchased from another
colliery. A tank wagon once used to carry acid has been adapted to
spray weedkiller on the track.

The Swansea and Mumbles tram came to a bad end. It was obtained in circumstances of inexperienced and optimistic enthusiasm, but its condition deteriorated over the years as persons prepared to maintain it failed to materialize. By 1970 its condition was
so bad that trust members voted to scrap it. The bogies with
electrical equipment were saved and the body burned.

To burn a preserved vehicle not unnaturally provoked criticism.
The moral is that if a railway preservation group finds that, in
attempting to maintain all its acquisitions, it has bitten off more

9 More industry. *Upper:* S & K L Rly, 0–4–2ST *Premier* waits at Kemsley Down; members are building coal stage and locomotive shed. (Author.) *lower* Leighton Buzzard Narrow Gauge Railway vertical boiler locomotive *Chaloner* stands at Page's Park. (Author.)

10 *upper* Fireman and blockman exchange train staffs at Brynglas, Talyllyn Railway. (J. F. Rimmer.)
lower Fireman's view of Signal and Telegraph Department at work, Festiniog Railway. (R. G. Roscoe.)

than it can chew—and Middleton is not alone—it should find
someone else who can look after them before they deteriorate too
much to be restored.

The Middleton Railway has about two miles of track in total.
Usually only one engine is in use, but the single line token, which
covers the whole railway, can be divided into parts for different
sections if needs be. The railway has public liability insurance
cover to £100,000.

There are no permanent staff on the railway—it is operated and
maintained entirely by volunteers. Annual subscription to the
trust is £1·25; there are only about 300 members. Most live
locally and Leeds University still provides a strong contingent.
Though total membership is low, the proportion of active membership is high—as many as 100 individuals help on the line at
least two or three times a year.

The thirteen-man committee of the Middleton trust, elected by
members, includes traffic manager, mechanical engineer and civil
engineer. Permanent way improvement has occupied much
volunteers' time, for they inherited a dilapidated-track problem
approaching that of the Talyllyn with the added complication
that, being standard gauge, materials were twice as big and heavy.
It takes at least two men to lift a full-size railway sleeper. Nevertheless in 1962 a new private siding was built.

On the mechanical engineering side, biggest jobs have been to
install a replacement boiler on a steam crane, and to make a new
smoke-box for *Matthew Murray*. All work on stock has to be done
in the open, but a wooden shed has been built as stores and workshop for small jobs. It says much for the enthusiasm of Middleton
members that they are able to run the railway under such circumstances and in such unprepossessing surroundings.

The Worth Valley Railway

The pleasant thing about the Worth Valley Railway is that it is a complete small branch line. It starts, as all good branch lines should, from a main line junction through which expresses to Scotland pass. Not so many as formerly, but they still do. Its route first threads an industrial town, then gains a rural winding valley. It includes two short tunnels, two level crossings, a viaduct, assorted bridges and several small intermediate stations. It finishes at a station which is laid out like a terminus for the simple reason that it has always been just that. There are no rusting rails to beckon through the grass towards A, no vague hopes of extensions to B.

The railway is standard gauge and a manageable 4¾ miles long, though frequent stations and sinuous course make it seem longer. It is run by Keighley and Worth Valley Light Railway Ltd., which is controlled by the Keighley and Worth Valley Railway Preservation Society. Together these form the largest entirely voluntary organization of its kind—they have no paid staff—and they also claim the largest and most varied collection of steam locomotives and rolling stock in Britain. The railway tends to be regarded as a place to display these in action. It also provides a local transport service with diesel rail-buses, though these see regrettably little custom. Their fares are fixed at a higher level than competing road buses, as a result of a five-year agreement made in 1968 with the local bus company—the price of its not objecting to Worth Valley light railway orders.

The main-line junction is Keighley, on the Leeds–Carlisle line. It was in 1971 the only station shared by trains of both British Rail and a preserved railway: Worth Valley trains use platform four. The line runs southwards with stations at Ingrow (1¼ miles from Keighley), Damems (2 miles), Oakworth (3 miles) and Haworth (3¾ miles); the terminus is Oxenhope. Some pronunciations, for non-Northerners: Keighley, first syllable pronounced *Keith*;

Damems, first syllable *Dam*; Haworth, first syllable *How* as in
How-do-you-do.

Oxenhope is 320 ft. higher than Keighley and the line rises
continuously. Its steepest gradient is 1 in 58 with a stretch of 1 in
46, where it leaves Keighley station, and there are long stretches
of 1 in 60 and 1 in 68. This means that engines work hard and are
heard to do so.

Keighley town has stone-built, soot-begrimed mills and mill
chimneys to remind visitors that they are in the Yorkshire woollen
district. Once in the country after leaving Ingrow the railway runs
near the bottom of its valley—it appears more rural than the
ordnance survey map suggests, for villages are hidden behind
brows of hills. Near the railway, stone walls enclose pocket
handkerchief-sized fields which slope steeply upwards on either
side.

This is the country of *The Railway Children*, or rather of television and film versions of that delightful story—both were made on
the Worth Valley Railway, in 1968 and 1970 respectively. Oakworth station, which featured extensively in the film, with its own
name, is restored to Victorian appearance.

Headquarters of the line are at Haworth station. Most of the
locomotives and rolling stock, when not in use, are stored in the
goods yard here, though some are at Oxenhope. The collection can
be inspected for 5p admission fee, which covers both sites.

From the bridge which crosses the railway at the south end of
Haworth goods yard a cobbled road leads uphill. As it climbs it
becomes steeper and steeper, narrower and narrower. At the top
(a shorter route for pedestrians starts from the foot-bridge at the
station) lies huddled together the old village of Haworth. Here
lived the literary Brontë family. Their parsonage home is now
a museum.

Trains run all year round on the Worth Valley Railway. In 1971,
from the beginning of April to the end of September they ran
every Saturday and Sunday, on bank holiday Mondays and Tues-
days, and also on Wednesdays in June, July and August. On other
weekdays there was no service except in August when a shuttle
service ran between Haworth and Oxenhope only. The summer
operating pattern tends to alter each year. A similar shuttle service
runs on winter Sundays; on winter Saturdays a diesel rail-bus

operates, over the whole line, with once-a-month steam services. At other times of the year a rail-bus works the first two or three return trips in the morning for local passengers, and steam trains run for the rest of the day.

Over the whole line, the minimum service in a day is four return trips; the maximum scheduled service of nine return trips was increased in 1971 to 13 by unadvertised extra trains. The fare for a round trip over the whole line from any station was 30p by steam train, 20p by rail-bus. Journey time from Keighley to Oxenhope is 23 minutes by rail-bus, 25 minutes by steam train. On summer Saturday evenings in 1971 ran the *Railway Children*'s trains— well-patronized specials formed of locomotives and coaches which appeared in the film.

Keighley is served by long-distance BR trains from London, Leeds, Morecambe and Glasgow. Sometimes passengers must change at Leeds or Skipton. There are local trains from Bradford which may be discontinued. At Keighley, Worth Valley trains connect with those of BR. There are no through bookings from BR stations to Worth Valley stations, nor are there at present any through excursions; but excursions sometimes run as far as Keighley for passengers to visit the Worth Valley line.

There are many bus services to both Keighley and Haworth; but public transport from Lancashire had deteriorated and was poor in 1971. In 1972 the Calderdale Omnibus Undertaking based on Halifax was operating an improved bus service from Hebden Bridge and Todmorden, meeting BR trains from Manchester at those places, as an experiment. There are car parks at Oxenhope, Haworth and Oakworth stations and 50 yards from Keighley station—that at Haworth tends to get overcrowded.

Many but by no means all of the locomotives on the Worth Valley Railway have associations with the North of England. In the summer of 1971 there were 30 steam locomotives on the railway of which 12 were used regularly and a further 6 occasionally on passenger trains. The remainder were either awaiting overhaul or else small locomotives, museum pieces rather than motive power, sometimes used to give foot-plate rides at Haworth. It is intended that all locomotives should be restored to working condition.

As a matter of policy, none of the steam locomotives belongs to Keighley and Worth Valley Light Railway Ltd. Nine of them belong to the preservation society and most of the remainder are owned either by individuals, by groups of members or by societies or the trustees of funds set up to preserve them. In 1970, independently owned locomotives hauled 67 per cent of trains.

Largest locomotives at the time of writing are two LMS class five 4–6–0s, numbers 5025 and 45212. While on British Railways, the latter was the last steam locomotive to haul a passenger train in regular service, in 1968. She was then bought by the society, with the aid of loans from members, for £3,000. Other locomotives often used include No. 72, an 0–6–0T built in America during the second world war for the US Army Transportation Corps and subsequently purchased by the Southern Railway, and 41241, a 2–6–2T built in 1949 to LMS design. Locomotives of its class were often used on the Worth Valley line in BR days. Three large and powerful 0–6–0 saddle tanks built in the early fifties for Stewarts and Lloyds steelworks have an uncouth appearance which has gained for them at Haworth the nickname 'Uglies'. The Worth Valley kindly gave me a foot-plate ride on one of them: a great chunky basic locomotive which took four coaches up the steep gradients as though they were feathers, with a blast of heat from the open firedoor enough to scorch the trousers of anyone rash enough to stand in front of it.

Locomotive No. 42700, an LMS 2–6–0, is part of the national collection of railway relics, on loan to the Worth Valley. It has sometimes been used to haul trains. Small locomotives used on the shuttle service between Haworth and Oxenhope include 0–6–0Ts which formerly ran on the Manchester Ship Canal's railway system and a Peckett 0–4–0 saddle tank which once shunted for the North Western Gas Board.

Experiences of two private locomotive owners stand for the others. Both locomotives were built for the Midland Railway. Class 1F 0–6–0T No. 1708 is one of a large class of locomotives, some of which formerly worked on the Worth Valley branch. With four others it outlived the rest to shunt sidings at Staveley Iron Works, in accordance with an agreement made for 100 years in 1866. When the agreement terminated the locomotives were withdrawn.

In the meantime, in September 1964, BR had quoted to the newly-formed Midland Railway 1F Locomotive Fund a price of

£875 for one of these locomotives when withdrawn. Twelve months later the price had increased to £1,250. After intervention by the A.R.P.S. it reverted to £875. No. 1708 came to Haworth in June 1967—needing an overhaul. It was Easter 1971 before she entered service, and then not on a regular basis.

The second locomotive is an 0–6–0 goods locomotive of class 4F: one of a very numerous class designed and built by the Midland Railway and, after the grouping, built in greater numbers still by the LMS. In 1965 the Midland 4F Preservation Society was formed: BR quoted £1,900 for either of their only two locomotives of the class remaining, for payment within three weeks. This the society could not meet—so the locomotives were sold for scrap and cut up. The society then selected No. 43924, last survivor of the Midland batch. She too had been sold for scrap: to Woodham Bros. of Barry, South Wales, with usual proviso that she should not be re-sold. Between them the A.R.P.S. and the society were able to obtain permission from BR for Woodham Bros. to re-sell her to the society. She was the first of many locomotives to be rescued from Barry. In 1968 she came to Haworth; by June 1970 restoration was far enough advanced for steam trials, and late in 1971 she entered service.

Lest it appear that British Railways sometimes behaved badly towards prospective purchasers of steam locomotives, it is only fair to add that they received a great many enquiries without being able to tell whether enquirers were responsible persons, able to raise funds, or even adult.

There are three diesel locomotives on the Worth Valley Railway and two four-wheeled diesel rail-buses. The latter were built in Germany in 1958 for British Railways as part of a too-little-and-too-late attempt to halt decline of branch-line traffic. They now belong to Keighley and Worth Valley Light Railway Ltd. and recall to the author travels on German branch lines in 1954 where such vehicles were already commonplace.

Coaches used regularly on passenger trains are numbered in the KWVLR's own series from 1 to 13 and 21 to 23 (most other vehicles retain pre-preservation numbers). Because the number of coaches that can be hauled up Worth Valley gradients by even a class five 4–6–0 is limited to six, to carry the crowds high capacity coaches have to be used. They include several non-corridor coaches built by BR for King's Cross suburban trains, and three Metropolitan Railway coaches intended, when first preserved, for the Westerham Branch in Kent. When the scheme to reopen that branch fell through they were transferred to the Worth Valley.

Two Pullman cars, an LNER buffet car and an LNER observation car are too heavy, in relation to the small number of passengers they carry, to run regularly although they sometimes appear with other corridor coaches in lightly loaded trains. There are two bogie saloons once used by railway officers on tours of inspection. One of these, built in 1871 for the locomotive superintendent of the North Eastern Railway, featured in *The Railway Children* as 'the old gentleman's coach' and is claimed to be the oldest standard-gauge passenger coach in service. Several elderly four- and six-wheeled coaches are museum exhibits. Like the locomotives, many coaches are independently owned. Full details of rolling stock appear in *Keighley and Worth Valley Railway Stockbook*.

Goods stock includes a recently acquired bogie well-wagon. Permanent way volunteers find its low deck valuable when loading heavy track materials from ground level. A diesel crane is used on track repairs, to lift signal posts, etc. Ballast, rails, sleepers and rolling stock materials are delivered in BR wagons which run on to the branch.

So far as locomotive and rolling stock liveries are concerned, the Worth Valley line appears to visitors a riot of gorgeous hues. In theory the policy is that locomotives should be painted an authentic livery; that is, one in which they ran at some earlier stage in their career. That the policy is often defeated is due partly to demands by film companies for photogenic but spurious liveries; partly to preferences by private owners for special liveries which the railway company does not veto unless they are outrageous; and partly to the fact that the policy does not apply to industrial locomotives anyway. So in 1971 BR standard class four 2–6–4T No. 80002 was restored to the full BR livery of a few years ago, even lettered *British Railways* although owned by the KWVRPS; Lancashire & Yorkshire Railway 0–6–0 No. 957 was in pale green and a GWR 0–6–0 pannier tank in brown, fictitious liveries in which they appeared in *The Railway Children*; class five No. 45212 was in BR's former livery for steam locomotives but with the Worth Valley's coat of arms in place of BR's crest (a solution which appeals to me); and several locomotives of both industrial and main-line origin were painted in various distinct liveries but lettered for the Worth Valley Railway although they belonged to private owners. The consequences of democracy! Livery of coaches had yet to be standardized. Former BR coaches were painted dark red.

One thing the 'complete branch line' lacked when taken over: any form of locomotive or carriage shed for storage and maintenance. In compensation it did have goods sheds at most stations and a very large one, intended for bulky woollen goods, at Haworth. This is now used as a repair shop. Locomotives and coaches in service stand outside it when not in use. The smoky, noisy business of preparing and running steam engines does not always, unfortunately, endear the Worth Valley Railway to its neighbours. But the railway does try to keep smoke and whistles down. Notices *Watch that Smoke* are instructions to enginemen rather than suggestions to visitors.

At Oxenhope two steel and asbestos sheds have been built to store and display vehicles temporarily out of use. The smaller of these has two tracks and holds half a dozen locomotives; it cost only £2,800, a very low price. The larger shed has three tracks and cost about £6,500. Both are to be extended, eventually. At Haworth a museum is to be built but here planning requirements are that it must be built of stone, despite the extra cost, to harmonize with the Brontë village.

On the maintenance side, re-tubing locomotives, I was told, had become something of a cottage industry at Haworth. Locomotives are lifted to remove wheels or axle-boxes for attention. One locomotive has had a new boiler fitted. Where equipment is not available for a particular job, the KWVRPS finds useful contacts in the local textile industry: textile machinery grew up in the same era as the steam locomotive and requires similar maintenance techniques.

The Worth Valley branch was built by the Keighley and Worth Valley Railway Company and opened in 1867. It passed successively into the ownerships of the Midland Railway (which had operated it from the start), the LMS and British Railways. In its day it prospered and served its valley well. In 1960 diesel trains replaced steam, but the line was considered uneconomic nevertheless. In December 1961 it was closed to passengers—although over

135,000 were carried in the last year—and in June 1962 it was closed to freight also.

By then the Keighley and Worth Valley Railway Preservation Society had already been formed in March at a public meeting in Keighley. The meeting, attended by 300 people, was called by G. R. Cryer and R. O. T. Povey, the former becoming the society's first chairman. Aim of the society was to preserve the Worth Valley Railway as a going concern. On 23 June, before the line closed completely, it was able to charter a special passenger train from Bradford to Oxenhope and back.

Though BR was helpful, negotiations for the railway were, as often, protracted. The society rented Haworth station as head-quarters and small relics museum. Early in 1965 the first locomotive acquired by the new regime was delivered by road; in March came the first locomotives and stock delivered by rail. These were the first trains to run on the line for nearly three years. Before they could do so, members had to replace more than 1,500 missing or rotten keys in the track. BR authorized members to repair track, fences, bridges and stations, and works trains and stock movements became familiar. Many thousands of people visited the museum.

Keighley and Worth Valley Light Railway Ltd. was incorporated on 8 February 1966, with a nominal capital of £10,000 in 1,000 ordinary shares of £10·00 each. The preservation society has a majority shareholding—by 1970 it held 487 shares out of the 615 which had been issued, or 79 per cent. Most of the other shareholders are active members of the society whose subscriptions to the company were much appreciated when money was being raised. Size of typical holdings is five shares, or £50·00. Other shareholders include nominees of the Locomotive Club of Great Britain (North West Branch) and the Gresley Society, which has three coaches and a locomotive on the railway. No dividend is paid or envisaged.

Independently of its shareholding the society has the right to appoint directors to the company: their number varies according to the total number of directors, but is never more than half. When the company has its full complement of ten directors, four are appointed by the society in this way. In practice, all company directors are society members.

Eventually the company arranged to purchase the line from a

point just outside Keighley station southwards, and to rent platform four at Keighley with adjoining track; BR were not prepared
to sell this section. The agreement made between the company and
the British Railways Board for purchase of the line provides for
payment of £45,000 by annual instalments of £1,800 for 25 years
from 1968, together with interest at £1,350 a year. Rent of platform four is £350 a year, on a 25-year lease. This makes the total
to be paid to BR each year £3,500. As security, the railway is
mortgaged to the BRB.

Light railway order and transfer order were obtained—after
objections by county council and local bus operator had been
met—and on 29 June 1968 the railway was reopened for passengers.

That year, 35,000 tickets were issued; in 1969, 60,000, in 1970,
70,000, and in 1971, 125,000. These are the numbers of bookings
made: to count journeys, as on other lines, would give a falsely
inflated idea of the number of visitors to the railway because many
make a round trip from Haworth which involves three journeys.
It is estimated that 95 per cent of all passengers are people out for
the day; 2 per cent are visitors taking holidays in the region; and
3 per cent are genuine local travellers. There is no freight or
parcels traffic.

Society membership was around 200 from 1962 to 1965 and
started to rise after rolling stock arrived at Haworth. In 1968 there
were 1,600 members and in 1971, 2,400. About 5 per cent of them
take an active part in running the railway, and most of these live
in Lancashire or the West Riding of Yorkshire. The annual subscription is £1·00 which entitles members to three free passes and
half-fare travel at all other times. With the potential of the line for
local transport, unlimited free travel, usual on other preserved
lines, would here make the membership subscription an excessively cheap season ticket.

It is something of a surprise to Worth Valley people that they
do manage entirely with voluntary staff—they anticipated lasting
perhaps six months from opening before taking paid staff on. One
effect of the all-volunteer organization is that the railway is run as
much to satisfy staff as passengers.

The function of general manager, in the long term, is performed
by a joint management committee drawn from both company and
society. In thoroughly democratic fashion, its meetings are open

to members to observe. Another joint committee deals with finance. The society is run by a council which has sub-committees to deal with rolling stock (locomotives, carriages, wagons and their maintenance), civil maintenance (track, bridges, boundary walls), station management (including buildings) and sales.

Smart station gardens are looked after by a group of members known to friends as the 'Parks and Cemeteries Department'.

'General manager' for the day, weekend or week is the Responsible Officer, one of a dozen senior members who fill this position in rotation. He sees that all functions smoothly, stations are staffed and properly run, and extra trains are put on if needed, and endeavours to retrieve the situation in event of a locomotive failure. To operate the line when a full service is running takes about 30 people. Locomotives run with a crew of three: the third man is a youngish member who cleans the locomotive in the morning, helps work points in the afternoon and generally gains foot-plate experience before moving up to fireman. Rail-buses are driven and maintained by a separate group of members to the steam drivers.

Since increasing traffic needed a more frequent service than could be provided by one train shuttling to and fro, and each terminus has only one platform, members have had to install a loop for two trains to cross at the half-way point near Damems. It was built remarkably quickly: the final decision to put it in was made in January 1971 and the loop was usable by May. A mechanical excavator prepared the site, digging ten feet deep in the process, and hard work by civil maintenance volunteers followed. The loop absorbed 300 tons of ballast, and is long enough to accommodate a class five 4–6–0 and six coaches. For its first season, the D.O.E. authorized use of flag signals to cross trains; subsequently it is to be fully signalled. The only other signals on the line protect level crossings. The railway is worked as either one or two sections each with one engine in steam; train staff(s) are carried. Keighley station is outside the single line and under control of a hand signalman. An omnibus telephone links all stations—since copper wire was stolen, steel wire is now used.

Division of income and responsibilities between society and company is clear cut. Society income is mainly derived from subscriptions, entrance fees to Haworth yard and sales. The sales department, with the slogan 'Sales preserve steam', has sales

counters for postcards, books etc. at Haworth, Keighley and
Oxenhope. The society retains main responsibility for providing
rolling stock. The company's income comes from fares and rents
of property (such as the goods shed at Oxenhope, still occupied by
tenants under a lease granted by BR) and from filming fees. *The
Railway Children* is far from being the only film made on the railway. The company has to pay the costs of operating the railway:
water, coal, insurance, track repairs (over ten years, half the rail
on the whole line is to be replaced), maintenance of stock and
buildings, lubricating and fuel oil, etc. To meet the £3,500 due
each year to the BRB, the absence of a wages bill must be a help.
Coal and oil cost about £5,500 a year.

During the year March 1969 to March 1970, the first full year
of running, traffic receipts were £8,690, filming fees £2,325 and
operating profit £936. But making a large profit is not envisaged:
some years the company makes a loss, met by a grant from the
society.

The Ravenglass and Eskdale Railway

Travel on a train of the Ravenglass and Eskdale Railway is a unique experience. Passengers are borne through the open air between the magnificent hills of the English Lake District at the speed of a fast bicycle, without the effort, or a slow motor cycle, without the noise. No roof impedes views of heathery rocky crags above, outlined against deep blue sky; no need to watch the road distracts attention from miniature steam among the gorse and bracken below.

For the Ravenglass and Eskdale is a miniature railway. To attract custom, the gauge of its track was made only 15 in., and its locomotives have the proportions of full-size machines scaled down. When the driver takes his place, sitting at the front of the tender, his head and sometimes shoulders loom above the roof of a cab scaled for small midgets. This is not to suggest the locomotives do not do a worthwhile job of work—R & E trains carry as many as 250 passengers. The coaches seat people two abreast; although many are open-air, some, introduced in 1967, are fully enclosed. Only one other miniature railway (the Romney, Hythe and Dymchurch) exceeds the R. & E's length of seven miles, and none at all passes through such attractive scenery.

The railway starts at Ravenglass in Cumberland. Its terminus is adjacent to Ravenglass station on BR's Barrow to Carlisle line. Special trains to Ravenglass, sponsored by the R & E Railway or its preservation society, run from many parts of the country—even from London since main-line electrification accelerated trains enough to bring Ravenglass within range of a day excursion. Buses from Whitehaven and Millom call at Ravenglass and the site of the big railway's goods yard there is now a car park for the small one.

The Ravenglass and Eskdale Railway runs generally in a direction between east and north-east. As far as Irton Road station, which is 4¼ miles from Ravenglass and has a passing loop, the line follows the valley of the River Mite, overshadowed by Muncaster Fell. It then turns briefly south-east, enters the valley of the River

Esk and resumes its former direction past Eskdale Green station
(4¾ miles); a little further on the line encounters its steepest gradient, a short length of 1 in 36. Hills are now high on either side
of the valley. There is a halt at Beckfoot half a mile before the
terminus at Dalegarth is reached. Here are picnic place and grassy
car park beneath the trees by the river. Both termini have cafes
and souvenir shops and there is a railway letter service.

The number of journeys made over the Ravenglass and Eskdale
Railway has increased from 73,000 in 1961 (the first year of preservation) to 225,000 in 1971. This has not entirely endeared it to
those who like uncrowded Eskdale. But a small train is nevertheless much better than motor cars for large numbers of people to
enjoy fine scenery with least harm to it. The point is relevant also
to the Welsh lines but particularly to the R & E.

Most passengers on the R & E are holiday-makers and the high
summer time-table shows ten trains each way daily. Many of these,
in fact, are duplicated. The journey takes 40 minutes and the adult
fare from Ravenglass to Dalegarth was 30p single, 50p return in
1971. At ends of the season, trains run less frequently.

Even in winter there is a train—diesel hauled—every weekday.
It leaves Dalegarth at 7.45 a.m. and returns from Ravenglass at
4.35 p.m. Though it runs principally to carry railway employees
resident up the line, it is used also by local travellers, particularly
the 4.35 p.m. working, for there is now no other public transport
in Eskdale. Weekend trains throughout the winter are being considered.

It is remarkable that the R & E Railway seems to provide more
of a public transport service than any other preserved line, although larger equipment often appears more suitable. Booted and
rucksacked hill walkers are frequent passengers and on Saturdays
many visitors with their luggage travel on it to reach hotels and
guest-houses in Eskdale. An Outward Bound School uses the
railway for access by participants in its courses: this means special
trains for 120 boys with luggage once or twice a month. There is
some parcel traffic too—mainly perishables such as meat for scout
camps. And should you order roast duck at the Bower House Inn,
near Eskdale Green, its excellence is enhanced by the knowledge
that it was delivered, from Manchester, via the Ravenglass and
Eskdale railway.

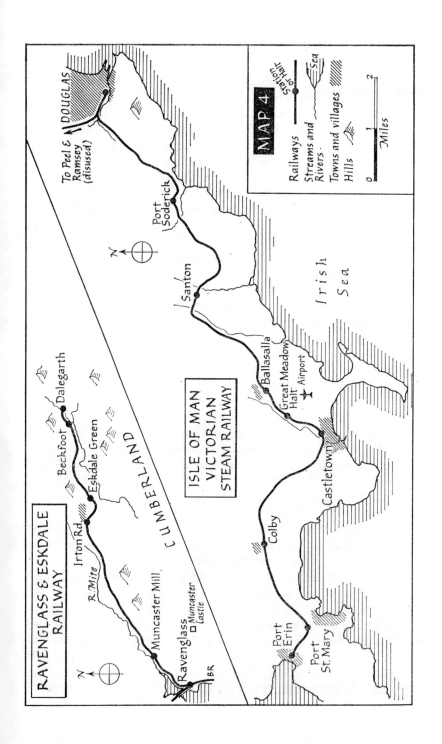

RAVENGLASS & ESKDALE RAILWAY

Dalegarth
Beckfoot
Eskdale Green
Irton Rd
R. Mite
Muncaster Mill
Muncaster Castle
Ravenglass
BR

CUMBERLAND

ISLE OF MAN VICTORIAN STEAM RAILWAY

To Peel & Ramsey (disused)
DOUGLAS
Port Soderick
Santon
Ballasalla
Great Meadow Halt
Airport
Castletown
Colby
Port Erin
Port St. Mary

Irish Sea

MAP 4

Station or Halt — Railways
Streams and Rivers
Sea
Towns and villages
Hills

Miles
0   1   2

The R & E was not always a miniature railway. Its early history
has, by coincidence, much in common with that of the Talyllyn.
Both lines were narrow gauge, built by mine or quarry owners to
carry minerals out of the hills to an exchange station with a coast-
wise standard-gauge line. Both were equipped with two locomotives, a few four-wheeled coaches and an assortment of wagons.
The Ravenglass & Eskdale Railway Co., however, was backed by
Whitehaven Iron Mines Ltd., the railway was opened in 1875,
had a gauge of three feet and carried iron ore. As with the Talyllyn,
the mining company soon failed, but mining continued in a limited
way and so did the railway. Where the R & E Company was worse
off was that it was heavily in debt to the contractor who had built
the line. It carried a little iron ore, a little granite, some ordinary
goods and passengers, and, at holiday times, any number of
holiday-makers. In this way it struggled on until 1908; an attempt
was then made at preservation (*sic*) by incorporating the Eskdale
Railway Co. to take it over, but failed for lack of finance. The line
was leased a couple of times to quarry owners; in 1912 the quarry
closed and in 1913 the railway followed suit. No Cumbrian Sir
Haydn Jones emerged to rescue them.

Two years later in 1915, however, the derelict railway was leased
again. This time the lease was different. It was to Narrow Gauge
Railways Ltd., for three years. Despite its name, NGR Ltd.
operated miniature railways, at seaside resorts and international
exhibitions; outbreak of war had handicapped both. One of its two
directors was W. J. Bassett Lowke of the famous model railway
firm. NGR Ltd. reduced the gauge of the line to 15 inches and
provided its own locomotives and rolling stock.

Today, few signs remain of the original 3 ft. gauge line. Over-
bridges built for its trains give ample headroom for passengers in
15 in. gauge open-air coaches. Some of the original rails are still in
use, though they are steadily being replaced as they wear out.
Perhaps a few will reach their centenary in 1975. And there is the
nickname of the railway, *Ratty*. Its origin seems forgotten.
D. Ferreira, present general manager, suggests that it derives from
Ratcliffe, the name of the contractor who built the original line.

The railway was reopened on the 15 in. gauge by stages. It
gradually obtained new and improved locomotives and rolling
stock and became popular with visitors. The lease was extended

11 *upper* Laying even 15 in. gauge track is a big job. Here it is laid
through the R & E Rly, Gilbert's Cutting, when new in 1964. (R & E R Co.)
lower The Dart Valley Railway had a bigger job still when run-round
loop, left, was laid in 1970. (Author.)

12 *upper* Hydraulic test. To test locomotive boiler for safety, Middleton Railway volunteer starts to pump up water pressure inside it. (Author.) *lower* View of cab. Bluebell Railway 9000 class 4–4–0 waits to leave Sheffield Park. (Author.)

until 1924; in that year Narrow Gauge Railways Ltd. acquired the freehold of the line and was itself taken over by shipowners Sir Aubrey Brocklebank and Henry Lithgow. Brocklebank, whose home was nearby, had loaned money to finance NGR Ltd. since 1917 and had developed Beckfoot granite quarry which brought the line much mineral traffic and revenue. A granite crushing plant was built at Murthwaite, $2\frac{1}{2}$ miles from Ravenglass, and railway and quarry companies later amalgamated. For many years, to avoid trans-shipment of crushed granite at Ravenglass, standard-gauge track was provided as far as Murthwaite—the miniature line ran down the middle of the standard gauge.

In 1948, after Lithgow's death (Brocklebank had died many years earlier) Narrow Gauge Railways Ltd., was sold to the Keswick Granite Co., to which company the granite quarry was a competitor. In 1953 the new owner closed the quarry, and in 1958 it put the railway (without the quarry) up for sale as a going concern for £22,500. Among those who negotiated unsuccessfully was Birmingham stockbroker and miniature railway enthusiast C. Gilbert. Another who had talks, which broke down over the price, was Sir W. Wavell Wakefield MP, who is today The Lord Wakefield of Kendal and chairman of the railway. His family connections with the Lake District go back several centuries and since the second world war he had been concerning himself with preserving its amenities and at the same time providing and preserving recreational facilities. To this end he had developed caravan sites so placed on the family estates that the caravans were hidden from general view, and had purchased, preserved and ensured continued operation of the steamer service on Ullswater Lake when it was about to cease functioning.

In 1960 the granite company announced that the railway would be auctioned, as a whole or in lots, on 7 September. Earlier that year the Ravenglass and Eskdale Railway Preservation Society had been formed and had raised £5,000 towards purchase of the railway. The imminent auction, with the possibility of the railway's being dismembered, brought the three parties I have mentioned together.

The winning bid at the auction, £12,000, was made by the late D. Robinson, clerk of Muncaster parish council, on behalf of the preservation society. The balance of the purchase price was put up by C. Gilbert and so were funds to maintain the railway through the ensuing winter while it had no traffic revenue. To own and run the railway the Ravenglass and Eskdale Railway Co. Ltd. was incorporated and registered on 30 March 1961. Guarantees were given to bankers by both Gilbert and Wakefield and the initial shareholders were these two with one share each.

Having put up the bulk of the cash, Gilbert was insistent that he should have control of the company. The remaining 9,998 shares of its nominal capital of £10,000 were allotted to him. To this Wakefield agreed on the understanding that if at any time Gilbert was to dispose of his interest, he would obtain first option to purchase. The society's £5,000 was represented by a loan-note. This loan is either interest-free or carries interest at a rate related to the dividend paid on ordinary shares. Up to the present the company has paid neither interest nor dividend. As a loan-note holder, the society is entitled to appoint a director to the board of the company. In September the first society nominee joined Gilbert and Wakefield on the company's board. Preservation and development of Ratty commenced.

In November 1968 came the sad death of C. Gilbert. The Ravenglass and Eskdale Railway Preservation Society found itself in a difficult position. In a will made in 1964, Gilbert had left his R & ER Co. Ltd. shares to the society; subsequent codicils revoked the bequest. The society considered both contesting the validity of the codicils (along with another beneficiary similarly placed) and also attempting to purchase the shares. It negotiated with the solicitors to Gilbert's executors, though it felt inhibited from pressing hard by the spirit of another clause in the will which directed that any beneficiary who pressed for payment would forfeit his legacy!

In April 1969, the executors without consulting their solicitors agreed to sell the shares to The Lord Wakefield of Kendal's family holding company, Battlefields (MTS) Ltd. In doing so they implemented Gilbert's undertaking that Lord Wakefield should have first option to purchase. The society, however, unaware of the latter point, filed a caveat to prevent transfer of the shares before validity of the codicils had been decided. It eventually transpired that the sale of the shares was in order, but the matter was not settled until December. In the meantime, for over a year, society members were in a state of uncertainty about the ownership of the railway they supported.

Although the late C. Gilbert led his R & E associates a bit of a dance, the railway would probably have been sold for scrap in 1960 but for his generosity. His memorial is Gilbert's Cutting, a deep cutting which enables the railway to avoid some sharp curves. He provided loan capital to pay for its construction.

The Ravenglass and Eskdale Railway Co. Ltd. is now a subsidiary of Battlefields. Its four directors, in addition to the chairman, include one appointed by the preservation society and two more from the society at the invitation of Lord Wakefield.

To secure the railway's future a tripartite agreement was made in December 1971 between Battlefields (MTS) Ltd., Ravenglass and Eskdale Railway Co. Ltd. and the Ravenglass and Eskdale Railway Preservation Society Ltd. (The society had incorporated itself as a guarantee company in 1961.) Its effect is to give the society first refusal to purchase either the physical assets of the railway or the share capital of R & ER Co. Ltd., according to circumstances, should Battlefields consider selling. In return the society agrees to loan three-quarters of its annual surplus to the railway. These loans would count towards eventual purchase price of the assets, and interest on them is earmarked for benefits to the railway's employees, former employees and their dependants.

It is the intention of the board of the Ravenglass and Eskdale Railway Co. Ltd. to preserve the railway in its present form by making it a viable commercial proposition. In this it has the support of the preservation society.

In 1960 there were only two steam locomotives on the railway: *River Esk*, a 2–8–2 built for it in 1923, and *River Irt*, an 0–8–2 rebuilt to miniature proportions in 1927 from 0–8–0T *Muriel*. She had been built originally, not as a miniature, in 1894 by that delightful Victorian engineer Sir Arthur Heywood for the Duffield Bank Railway, which he had constructed in his grounds to demonstrate that 15 in. was a practical minimum gauge for railways as transport. There are plans for her to revert to narrow-gauge rather than miniature appearance. Indeed the whole railway now tends towards fulfilment of the ideas of Heywood rather than Bassett Lowke.

Increasing traffic demanded another locomotive. While engines

suitable for Welsh narrow-gauge lines were hard to find, one for a
unique line like Ratty was non-existent. A new one had to be built.
She arrived in 1967, a 2–8–2 called *River Mite*, built by H. Clark-
son & Son of York with a boiler by J. & W. Gower and frames that
the railway had already available. She was paid for by the preservation society and remains its property, leased to the company. Her
total cost was £8,018 10s. 2d. This was raised by a locomotive
fund, supported temporarily by loans which have now been
repaid.

The two earlier locomotives were both painted green. Persistent
confusion among members of the public, who enquired after the
'little green engine' without appreciating that there were *two* of
them, led to a new livery of deep black for *River Esk* when she
needed repainting. *River Mite* is painted bright cherry-red. The
locomotives are named after the three rivers which flow into the
sea at Ravenglass. They burn coke instead of coal to keep down the
quantity of smuts which might get into open-air passengers' eyes
and hair.

There are various diesel locomotives, old and new, used on
morning and evening trains and on relief trains, when necessary,
during the day. Open-air coaches are used for scheduled trains
and closed coaches for reliefs when the weather is fine; when it is
wet, vice versa. Most coaches now in use have been built since
1960, the 14 aluminium-bodied closed coaches by contract and the
27 wooden-bodied open-air ones at Ravenglass. The numbers of
the latter indicate the dates of construction: e.g. coach No. 270,
the second to be completed in 1970.

Many improvements have been made to the track—the R & E
was the first preserved railway to use Jarrah sleepers—and to
stations. At Ravenglass the track layout has been improved and
other improvements are foot-bridge, signal cabin, signals, diesel
depot and a cavernous carriage shed.

The railway has a permanent staff of 13. Under the general
manager are chief engineer and operating foreman. Under these in
turn are, respectively, two engineers and a carpenter/carriage
builder, and drivers and guards; guards work on the track in
winter. Each steam locomotive has her own regular driver who
drives and fires single-handed; in winter he helps when his locomotive is overhauled. Temporary staff are employed in summer—

often students and society members—as diesel locomotive drivers, guards, and station staff. Staff in shops and cafés are seasonal also, often returning year after year. Volunteers from the preservation society work as guards in summer, and have working parties on the track in winter.

About 100 out of the society's total membership of around 1,500 take an active part on the railway. Local support for the railway is remarkable: in 1970 there were 170 members in the locality of Ravenglass, Eskdale and Irton, and more than half the total membership lives in north-west England. Members of area groups are active in publicizing the railway, distributing time-tables and attending exhibition stands. Annual subscription is £1·00 and members get unlimited free travel on the railway.

In the twelve months ended 31 March 1971, the R & ER Co. Ltd.'s total expenditure was £31,720 in which the principal items were salaries and wages, maintenance, depreciation, rates, interest payments and advertising. There was a net surplus of £322. Passenger receipts were £27,000, miscellaneous revenue from car parks, etc., was £2,120 and the surplus on catering (after deducting wages but not allowing for depreciation, etc.) was nearly £3,000.

The Ravenglass and Eskdale Railway has extensive plans for improvements. Awnings are to be provided over platforms at Ravenglass and Dalegarth. Continuous brakes, operated by compressed air and incorporating road vehicle components, are to be fitted to locomotives and coaches. A second new locomotive is planned for 1973—to be assembled at Ravenglass. Biggest plan of all is for an extension of the line from Ravenglass, first south and then east, for 2⅔ miles to Muncaster Castle. This is a stately home open to the public. Planning permission for the extension has already been received.

9　The Isle of Man Railway

Note. This chapter describes the Douglas to Port Erin line of the Isle of Man Railway up to the date at which it was written (early 1972). At that time the line was known as the Isle of Man Victorian Steam Railway; for important recent developments see appendix A.

Of all preserved railways that of the Isle of Man is least changed by preservation. In 1971 I found only superficial alterations since my last visit ten years previously, at which time the railway had still been part of the island transport system. No additions had been made to locomotives or rolling stock, no alterations had been made to buildings or track layouts. Elegant and shiny Beyer Peacock 2–4–0Ts still galloped along with heavy trains of holiday-makers, to the accompaniment of frequent ear-splitting whistles and much waving of flags.

Running 15½ miles from Douglas, capital of the island, to Port Erin at its south-western end, the railway offers the longest regularly scheduled steam train journey in the British Isles. As the adult return fare between the two termini is only 70p it is also very cheap. The gauge of the railway is 3ft. and the journey from one end to the other takes about one hour. There are stations *en route* at Port Soderick, Santon, Ballasalla, Castletown, Colby and Port St. Mary. At Douglas station a shop sells souvenirs, badges, slides and postcards.

The railway gets financial aid from the Manx government, in the interest of the tourist trade which is the island's main industry. The Isle of Man, which John Betjeman describes succinctly in *First and Last Loves*, is a much frequented holiday resort today, but it came into popular favour in Victorian times. The working masses of the North of England took to holiday-making in the Isle of Man with the same enthusiastic sense of adventure that their great-grandchildren now give to a visit to the Costa Brava. Douglas buildings have the architecture of Victorian cities without their overlay of grime: white brick hotels on the promenades retain pristine whiteness, and the red brick of Douglas station remains a very bright red. It is no small station, but an impressive terminus —like other stations on the island it was extended and expanded to cope with Victorian and Edwardian holiday crowds.

Almost as soon as they leave Douglas, trains meet the toughest bank on the railway, two miles of 1 in 65 and 1 in 70. The steepest gradient, however, is 1 in 60 rising in the opposite direction for half a mile between Santon and Port Soderick. The railway gives passengers glimpses of rocky coast on one side and distant hills on the other, but generally it runs through farms where fields are separated by banks topped with crimson fuchsia and linked by flimsy gates hung between grandiose stone gateposts—all of which are a reminder that one is more than half-way across the Irish Sea.

Although the Isle of Man is a Crown possession it is not part of the United Kingdom and enjoys a great deal of self-government. It has its own parliament, called Tynwald. The Isle of Man Railway Co. Ltd. was registered in the island in 1870, and has remained independent, unaffected by grouping or nationalization of British railways. The company built lines from Douglas to Peel (opened in 1873) and Port Erin (1874). Lines opened subsequently by the Manx Northern Railway from a junction at St. Johns, near Peel, to Ramsey, and by the Foxdale Railway from St. Johns to Foxdale, were taken over in 1904.

The railway company prospered until bus competition came in the late twenties. This it counteracted by buying out the bus operators and forming a subsidiary, Isle of Man Road Services Ltd., to run the bus services, which it still does. Eventually, as might be expected, the tail wagged the dog, but the railway survived an astonishingly long time. Over a million passenger journeys were made on it as recently as 1950. Then, as visitors became fewer and residents bought cars, train services were gradually reduced. During the winter of 1960 to 1961 the short section from St. Johns to Peel was closed except for occasional special trains. In the spring it was reopened but during the following and subsequent winters the longer section from St. Johns to Ramsey was closed. In 1965 extensive track repairs became necessary and for these to be done the whole system was closed on 13 November. But in a letter to shareholders the following January the chairman stated that the

directors had, to their regret, decided that trains had to cease
running because of lack of revenue and ever-increasing costs.

As long as the company owned the track it was obliged to maintain bridges, fences, etc. It obtained powers to dispose of assets
and surplus land.

In August 1966 the Manx Steam Railway Society was founded
on the island. A committee was appointed to investigate the
finance, material and organization needed to keep at least part of
the railway operating. After several months' work it concluded
that the sum needed to acquire and operate even part of the railway was far beyond what could be raised from members of a
supporters' society, and that help from the Isle of Man government would be needed.

However on 1 April 1967 the whole railway, including rolling
stock and most buildings, was leased by the company to the
Marquess of Ailsa whose intention appears to have been to reopen
the railway and operate it commercially as a tourist attraction. The
lease was for 21 years with option to purchase. The society altered
its name to Isle of Man Steam Railway Supporters' Association
and pledged its support.

On 3 June the railway was reopened at Douglas amid pomp and
ceremony. At first trains ran between Douglas, Peel and Ramsey.
On 10 July the Port Erin line was reopened as far as Castletown
and a halt near Ronaldsway airport established. Between Castletown and Port Erin a gas-main was being laid along the railway
—the track was reinstated during the 1968 season.

In 1967 the IOMR Co. Ltd. resumed payment of dividends to
preference shareholders and in 1968 to ordinary shareholders, in
each instance the first payments since 1964. But Lord Ailsa,
according to the *Railway Magazine*, stated after two seasons that
he could not run the railway without financial assistance. This was
eventually forthcoming as a subsidy from the Manx government of
£22,500 spread over three years, for operation of steam trains on the
Douglas to Port Erin line which offered most traffic. This scheme
was proposed by the Isle of Man Tourist Board and reinforced by
a large petition organized by the supporters' association. To operate
the line the Isle of Man Victorian Steam Railway Co. Ltd. was
registered, with the Marquess of Ailsa as chairman and two other
directors who were Isle of Man residents as required by Manx law.

The new company operated the Port Erin line successfully during the summers of 1969, 1970 and 1971, but in the spring of 1971 Lord Ailsa gave 12 months' notice to terminate his lease of the railway on 31 March 1972, the earliest date he could do so under its terms. On 20 October 1971, Tynwald approved a plan to preserve the Douglas to Port Erin line as an asset to the tourist industry. The Isle of Man Tourist Board was authorized to enter into a lease with the Isle of Man Railway Company from 1 April 1972 until 12 November 1974 (i.e., three summer operating seasons) at a rental of £9,000 a year for the two years ending 31 March 1974 and £5,265 for the remaining period. The lease covers use of the line including stations, rolling stock, locomotives and plant. The intention was for the line to be operated by the IOMVSR Co. Ltd., with a guarantee against losses, but this scheme did not reach fruition. As I write in February 1972 the latest news is that Tynwald has agreed that the tourist board should enter into an agreement with the Isle of Man Railway Co. for the latter to operate the line from 1 April 1972 until 12 November 1973, with power to extend the agreement until November 1974 should the railway company so agree.

In 1971, trains on the Port Erin line ran at Easter and then from mid-May to the end of September, daily except on Sundays. The peak service of five trains each way daily ran from 19 July to 27 August. The 1972 service is shown in appendix A. The holiday season in the Isle of Man is very short. The island is only 35 minutes by air from Liverpool or four hours by sea, so it is regrettable in my opinion that both air and sea schedules discourage out-of-season weekend visits because Friday and Sunday evening services are lacking. Otherwise good services are run to the Island by the Isle of Man Steam Packet Co. Ltd., which still operates genuine steamships, and Cambrian Airways Ltd. Not many of those arriving by air at Ronaldsway continued by train from Great Meadow Halt, those who did had the distinction of following, more or less, in the footsteps of Miss World. When the then holder of that title flew into the island in 1969, she (Australian Miss Penny Plummer) sensibly travelled on to Douglas by train, though in her instance a car was provided at the airport to take her to Castletown station. The halt was closed after 1971.

The railway's usual traffic is almost entirely holiday-makers 'from across', but while some go on it for the ride, others use the railway to reach the resort at which they are staying, or to get about the southern part of the island. Traffic is now on the increase again, with 103,623 journeys made in 1971. Special trains are popular with organizations, both visiting and local. It cost £35.00 in 1971 to hire a special from Douglas to Port Erin and back inside normal weekday working hours, at other times slightly more. There is very little local passenger traffic, but a few parcels are carried.

Besides the steam railway, the vintage Manx Electric Railway and Douglas horse trams are attractions to rail-conscious visitors. Locomotives are painted light green, carriages red and cream. There are about 30 carriages in use—some have the bodies of early four-wheelers mounted in pairs on bogie underframes, others are either orthodox compartment stock or handsome period saloons. Five locomotives were in regular use in 1971: No. 4 *Loch*; No. 10 *G. H. Wood*; No. 11 *Maitland*; No. 12 *Hutchinson*; and No. 13 *Kissack*. All were 2–4–0Ts; their dates of building range from 1874 to 1910. With the exception of *Hutchinson*, which was spare engine, all engines in use had their own regular crews. Other locomotives, in reserve or awaiting repair, were on view as exhibits. Two diesel railcars obtained by the IOMR Co. in 1961 from the County Donegal Railways were used for charter excursions and staff transport. Under the terms of the subsidy they are not used on regular trains. When lineside hedges need to be trimmed, a railcar propels a goods wagon carrying a hired farm tractor, to which is fitted mechanical hedge-cutting equipment.

The railway has a permanent staff of about 20 which increases to about 50 in summer. Some ten of the total are men employed by the IOMR prior to 1966. For example, the former signalman at Douglas comes out of retirement to work the 36-lever box there each summer. Under the general manager there are three departments: Permanent Way, headed by the permanent way inspector; Locomotive, headed by the locomotive superintendent who has 50 years' service; and Traffic, headed by Douglas station-master. Traffic staff work on maintenance in winter. Between 1969 and 1971 some 4,000 new sleepers (second-hand from British Rail, cut down to 6 ft. length) were laid in the track, and some new rail has been laid also.

The supporters' association with an adult annual subscription of £1·50 has a membership of about 550. Members voluntarily paint carriages, assist staff at stations and guards on trains, and in a few instances have been passed as guards themselves. The association gives no direct financial support to the railway but it does raise money through sale of goods. It also pays for advertisements on the Manx commercial radio station. There is no formal agreement between association and railway.

The railway is operated by train staff and printed card ticket under control of Douglas station-master. There were passing loops used in 1971 at Soderick, Ballasalla, Castletown and Colby. An omnibus telephone links stations and is maintained by the post office. Much use is made of whistles in operating the railway. For example, signals are not lowered until 'whistled off' by an approaching train, drivers blow the whistle as they approach level crossings, and three or more short sharp blasts are a request to the guard to apply brakes, for continuous brakes are not used. There is an extensive code of whistles for drivers to communicate with the signalman at Douglas as locomotives approach, leave or move about the station.

The British Department of the Environment has no authority over the railway, but it is affected by Isle of Man legislation which requires any railway in the island which has not carried passengers for six months to be examined, before re-use, by a government-appointed inspector.

For storage the railway is well endowed with locomotive sheds at Douglas and Port Erin, and carriage sheds at Douglas. For maintenance, the works at Douglas, intended to keep the stock of a more extensive system in repair with insular self-sufficiency, is equipped with a full if slightly elderly range of machinery. Here in 1968 and 1970 respectively new boilers, supplied by Hunslet Engine Co., were fitted to locomotives *Loch* and *Kissack*.

The Severn Valley Railway

A train on the Severn Valley Railway seems just like an ordinary train. Until, on reflection, you realize that no ordinary train you have seen or travelled on has been like this for quite a while. Severn Valley trains are the ordinary steam trains of ten or twenty years ago, not the diesel or electric trains of today. Most locomotives and coaches are relatively modern, examples of types that were common during the last years of steam on British Railways. They still seem familiar now. It is difficult to comprehend that class 8F 2–8–0 No. 8233, for instance, is the only working survivor of her class in Britain when as recently as 1964 there were 640 more engines like her.

The Severn Valley Railway is standard gauge and ran, in 1971, from Bridgnorth, Shropshire, southwards for $4\frac{1}{2}$ miles to Hampton Loade. It has plans to extend, of which more shortly. Half-way between Bridgnorth and Hampton Loade is a halt called Eardington. The railway is never far from the river of its name, and Hampton Loade proper is on the opposite bank to its station, to which it is connected by a small ferry, though the station is also accessible by a by-road on its own (west) side of the river. The steepest gradient on the line is 1 in 100.

There is a car park at Bridgnorth, and on busy days a field overlooking the station becomes car park and picnic place. By public transport the best approach to the railway is probably by train to Wolverhampton, whence there is an hourly bus service to Bridgnorth. At Bridgnorth station are information desk, a bookstall which also sells model railway goods and records, a licensed refreshment room—the licensee has been there continuously since BR days—and a buffet car, stationary but functioning.

The 1971 summer time-table showed train services at weekends and bank holidays from 10 April to 31 October, with from five to nine trains in each direction on each operating day. On Saturday mornings a diesel railcar made several journeys to take people

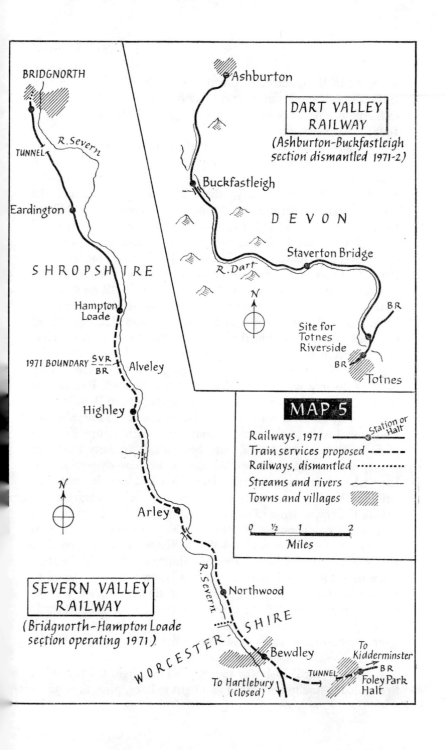

BRIDGNORTH

R. Severn

TUNNEL

Eardington

SHROPSHIRE

Hampton
Loade

1971 BOUNDARY $\frac{SVR}{BR}$ Alveley

Highley

N

Arley

**SEVERN VALLEY
RAILWAY**

(Bridgnorth-Hampton Loade
section operating 1971)

WORCESTER-SHIRE

R. Severn

Northwood

To Hartlebury
(closed)

Bewdley

TUNNEL

To
Kidderminster
BR
Foley Park
Halt

Ashburton

**DART VALLEY
RAILWAY**

(Ashburton-Buckfastleigh
section dismantled 1971-2)

Buckfastleigh

DEVON

Staverton Bridge

R. Dart

N

Site for
Totnes
Riverside

BR

BR

Totnes

MAP 5

Railways, 1971 —————— ●— Station or Halt
Train services proposed - - - - -
Railways, dismantled ············
Streams and rivers ——————
Towns and villages ▨▨▨

0   ½   1   2
Miles

shopping in Bridgnorth. In practice many extra trains were run, and trains ran continuously every day for a fortnight from 24 July to 8 August. Adult return fare for the whole journey was 30p in 1971; it has since risen.

The railway was first opened in 1862. It was part of the line built by the Severn Valley Railway Co. to link Shrewsbury with Worcester; this line ran from Shrewsbury via Bridgnorth, Bewdley and Stourport to Hartlebury, where it made a junction with the Kidderminster–Worcester main line. The Severn Valley Railway Co.'s line was at first leased to and worked by the West Midland Railway Co., but both companies were amalgamated with the Great Western Railway Co. in the early 1870s. A branch from Bewdley direct to Kidderminster was opened in 1878.

These lines all passed to the Western Region of BR on nationalization and were transferred to the London Midland Region in 1963. Through trains between Shrewsbury and Bewdley ceased the same year and part of the line, including the section which is now the preserved Severn Valley Railway, was closed completely.

At a meeting in Kidderminster on 6 July 1965 the Severn Valley Railway Society was formed. Its aim was a Bluebell Railway for the Midlands. At this time the line northwards from Bewdley was still used by goods trains as far as Alveley colliery, a mile short of Hampton Loade station; while from Bridgnorth in the direction of Shrewsbury track had already been lifted. A party from the society inspected the disused Alveley to Bridgnorth section and liked what it saw—except that demolition had already started at Bridgnorth. After a telegram sent by the society chairman to British Railways, demolition was suspended for negotiations. This remarkable co-operation by BR has continued, on the whole, as a characteristic of the Severn Valley Railway to the present day. BR staff occupy positions of responsibility on the SVR in their spare time. Of more immediate importance was BR's response to requests to lease or buy the line. Application for a lease was rejected, but an offer of £25,000 for land, track and buildings, made after valuation by an estate agent, was accepted. It was not a high figure, but in those early days it took the society until February 1967 to raise the £2,500 deposit.

Later that year British Railways applied for a light railway order, to enable the line to be worked as a light railway, prior to application for a transfer order. It attracted objections from local authorities: Highley Parish Council and Shropshire County Council. The former was concerned with improvements to road bridges near Eardington, and the latter planned a Bridgnorth bypass to cut across the railway south of the town. A public local enquiry was held in Shrewsbury in October 1968. Subsequently the inspector recommended to the Minister of Transport that the L.R.O. should be granted.

The Minister did not agree—because of the extra cost to public funds of building the bypass bridge. The objection concerning Eardington bridges was not sustained. So far as the bypass was concerned, the parties were requested to meet again. The solution that emerged was that the Severn Valley Railway promoters agreed that when the bypass was made the railway would either pay for a bridge or allow the line to be cut. On this basis the L.R.O. was made for the section Bridgnorth to milepost $144\frac{1}{2}$, near Alveley, and a transfer order followed in May 1970.

The previous December, members and activities of the Severn Valley Railway Society had passed to the Severn Valley Railway Co. Ltd., a guarantee company incorporated in May 1967. Following the light railway transfer order in favour of the SVR Co. Ltd., the railway was reopened on Whit-Saturday, 23 May 1970. Trains ran at weekends.

After only three weekends they had to stop again, until the conveyance for the purchase was completed and the price paid in full. The balance still due was £20,500; this was raised in two weeks, £14,500 by donations and £6,000 by loans. Quite an achievement. Trains started again on 27 June.

Meanwhile, in January 1969, the line south from Alveley to Bewdley had been closed, following closure of Alveley Colliery, and in January 1970 the surviving passenger services from Bewdley, to Hartlebury and Kidderminster, were withdrawn. Bewdley station was completely closed, though the far ends of both Hartlebury and Kidderminster lines are still used to provide rail access to a power-station at Stourport and a sugar factory at Foley Park respectively.

All this has left the Severn Valley Railway with two big problems. Firstly, if the closed lines south of Alveley are dismantled, it will lose its connection with the main railway system. Secondly, if

it is unable to raise the money for a bridge for Bridgnorth bypass
—and plans are that the bypass will be built before 1975—its line
will be cut and its principal station stranded on less than a mile of
railway. Estimates of the cost of the bridge range from £10,000 to
£80,000, depending on whether a suitable second-hand railway
bridge can be located, and re-erected partly by volunteers, or
whether landscaping needs will demand a new bridge blending
with its environment, built by contractors. The higher figure
seems the more probable.

The company's response was bold. It is endeavouring to purchase the line south from Alveley through Bewdley and as far as
Foley Park, with the hope of eventually extending into Kidderminster. From Bridgnorth to Foley Park will give a line 15 miles
long.

Assuming success in purchasing the southern section, the railway will have an extensive line to run even if, at the worst, it is cut
by the bypass. What is more likely is that the longer line would
have sufficient assets against which to borrow money to pay for a
bridge, and increased revenue from which to pay interest and
repayments on the money borrowed. First, however, cash has to
be raised, to purchase the southern section, estimated at £75,000,
with another £35,000 needed for working capital.

By the time these words are published, the railway's success or
otherwise in this plan will probably be history known to the reader.
I state here intentions as they stand early in 1972.

The assets of the existing guarantee company will pass to a new
company: Severn Valley Railway (Holdings) Ltd., a public
company limited by shares. The authorized capital of the new
company is £150,000; of this, £40,000 is allotted to the guarantee
company in return for its members' interest in the existing line;
the remaining £110,000 is to be offered for public subscription in
stages with priority given to guarantee company members. It is
not anticipated that there will be dividends before 1975; indeed
an annual subsidy is promised by Bridgnorth Rural District
Council on condition the line is reopened to Kidderminster.

Chairman of the boards of both Severn Valley Railway Co. Ltd.
and Severn Valley Railway (Holdings) Ltd. is Sir Gerald Nabarro
M.P. Total of directors on the board of the new company is to be
about nine; they will include two nominated by the guarantee com-

13 *upper* Final polish for *The Earl*, Welshpool and Llanfair Light Railway. To the right is Llanfair Caereinion's new locomotive shed. (Author.)
lower Coal is loaded into bunker of 0–6–0 pannier tank locomotive at Bridgnorth, Severn Valley Railway. (Author.)

14 *upper* Platform scene at Bridgnorth with GWR coaches, Severn Valley Railway. (Author.)
lower Platform scene at Buckfastleigh with *Devon Belle* observation car, Dart Valley Railway. (Author.)

pany. The holdings company will decide policy; below it will be the guarantee company board, and a small nucleus of full-time staff will gradually be built up.

Among the new company's most urgent tasks will be to set up extensive sheds and works for locomotives and carriages. At present both live in the open. The goods shed at Bridgnorth is used to repair locomotives.

In 1971, the goods shed and sidings at Bewdley, too, were being rented, and the shed is used for carriage maintenance and painting. Shabby when they arrive, coaches are gradually being restored to their original liveries with a very high standard indeed. They are painted by amateurs, led by a member who is a signwriter by trade and had access to original formulations of paint supplied to railway companies. Most coaches are bogie corridor vehicles of GWR or LMS design, now privately owned. They include a GWR 'special saloon' which ran in the royal train and a luxurious 'super saloon' built for boat trains from Paddington to Plymouth in the days when transatlantic liners called there. Most goods wagons on the line do belong to the company and are used on maintenance trains. Some are restored to former railway company colours, some represent 'private owners' in the old sense, that is, of mining or quarrying concerns which had their own railway wagons, and some are lettered SV for the Severn Valley Railway.

In 1971 there were five locomotives used frequently on passenger trains. The LMS class five 4-6-0 No. 45110 was named *RAF Biggin Hill* in September in memory of the RAF Biggin Hill wartime airport and the Battle of Britain. There was an impressive ceremony which included a fly-past. Two 2-6-0s (class two No. 46443 and class four No. 43106) belong to the last generation of LMS-designed locomotives and were built after nationalization. The class 8F 2-8-0, built for heavy freight trains, has already been mentioned. No. 5764, an 0-6-0 pannier tank, is one of those typical Great Western locomotives, purchased by London Transport to haul maintenance trains over the Underground at night when electricity was switched off. She came to Bridgnorth in 1971 in running order as London Transport No. L95.

By courtesy of the SVR, I was able to spend a day on her footplate as a sort of extra man to the driver and fireman to see how a full-size standard-gauge locomotive compared with the 2 ft.-gauge

locomotives to which I am accustomed. Things were nothing like
as massive as I anticipated—I believe the opposite holds good for
standard-gauge men who visit the narrow-gauge lines. Locomotives
for both are designed round people of the same size.

In addition to these, two other locomotives—War Department
o-6-o saddle tank No. 193 and GWR o-6-o No. 3205—saw some
use, and two handsomely repainted industrial o-6-oTs shunted
and gave foot-plate rides at Bridgnorth. Shoppers' train services
were operated by GWR diesel railcar No. 22, of a type familiar on
the line before closure, and a small diesel locomotive was used on
works trains. Nine other steam locomotives awaited entry into
service.

The only locomotive owned by the SVR Co. Ltd. is No. 193.
The others are independently owned and the company has entered
into formal agreements with their owners. As an example, the
agreement for No. 8233, which is owned by the Stanier 8F Locomotive Society Ltd. (by guarantee), gives the SVR Co. Ltd.
exclusive right to operate her and retain all revenue from doing so.
In return the Severn Valley company provides fuel and locomotive crews and pays for maintenance and boiler insurance.

Locomotives are restored to former owners' liveries. That there
are both GWR and LMS factions among SVR members is
demonstrated by the origins of locomotives and rolling stock—but
while the GWR is predominant on the coaching side, the LMS
predominates where locomotives are concerned! Railways operated
jointly by LMS and GWR were once a feature of Shropshire so,
although the Shrewsbury–Worcester line was not one of them, the
mixture has its precedent.

Other stock includes a steam crane and complete breakdown
train for emergencies and a Matisa ballast tamper for maintaining
track mechanically.

To meet insurance requirements, all volunteers working on the
railway must be Severn Valley members, even if they are at work
on privately owned locomotives. The only full-time employees in
1971 were the general manager and his secretary, though car park
tickets were sold by part-time staff and maintenance of lineside
hedges was being let out to contract. Passenger traffic at times was
intense, necessitating trains as long as eight or ten coaches, and
trying to cross the foot-bridge at Bridgnorth in the wrong direction

just before a train was due out was like trying to go up the down escalator! In 1971, passengers made 171,095 journeys; the previous year the figure was 63,660. Even before the railway was open, steam galas at Bridgnorth station attracted big crowds—as many as 10,000 people on one occasion. Bridgnorth, a picturesque town with the river as well, has long been a place for inhabitants of the nearby Wolverhampton/Birmingham area to go to for a day out. At Bewdley, a wild life park is planned adjacent to the railway. There is no freight traffic—a project for an oil depot which would have meant bulk oil trains did not come to fruition—though there are hopes for some when the line is open through from Foley Park.

In 1971 the railway was operated with wooden train staffs for sections Bridgnorth to Hampton Loade, and Hampton Loade to Alveley—the latter being used only by works trains. GWR signals, and signal boxes, were being restored, and electric train staff equipment is being installed. An automatic telephone system is already working, with exchange at Bridgnorth. The Severn Valley Railway Co. Ltd. (by guarantee) had an adult annual subscription of £1·50 and about 3,000 members; on typical weekends about 100 of them worked voluntarily on the railway. There are five local branches.

The accounts of the Severn Valley Railway Co. Ltd. for ten months ending 31 October 1971—which include the railway's second operating season—show gross traffic receipts of £20,998, bookstall sales of £11,557 and catering sales of £11,110. Surpluses on these three items were respectively £7,994 (i.e., traffic receipts less working expenses), £3,810 and £1,651. Other income included subscriptions at £4,187.

The Dart Valley
Railway

Note. This chapter describes the DVR's Totnes to Buckfastleigh line. For details of its recently acquired Paignton to Kingswear line, see appendix A.

To visit the Dart Valley Railway is like finding oneself on a branch line of the Great Western. It is as though one had stepped back 40 years, say those who remember such lines in their Indian summer of the 1930s. The dark green engines are of distinctive Great Western design, the coaches are all coloured Great Western chocolate and cream and the whole railway has the GWR's air of gentlemanly spaciousness. It is set in pleasant and appropriate West Country surroundings.

The all-Great Western appearance of the railway gives it an identity, something often lacking elsewhere, which makes it attractive to visitors whether or not they appreciate the reason. And a great many visitors do come, with Torbay resorts close at hand. In 1969, the first season after reopening, some 240,000 journeys were made over it, by far the highest first-season figure for any preserved railway. After a slight fall in 1970, passenger journeys in 1971 returned to their former level.

This popularity confirms the early contention of promoters of The Dart Valley Light Railway Ltd. that there would be no lack of passengers. Because of this they considered that the preserved railway would be commercially viable and make a reasonable return for investors. It was financed by issue of shares and loan stock. That it has yet to produce the expected return results from a feature at first considered an advantage: the A38 trunk road.

The light railway company's object was to purchase or lease the closed branch which left the main Exeter to Plymouth line at Totnes, Devon, and ran via Buckfastleigh to Ashburton. Over the latter section it paralleled the A38. In full view of the many holiday-makers who drive that way would be the trains themselves, better than any poster. Unfortunately the road is so busy that a scheme to provide a dual carriageway by using much of the track-bed of the railway has, after a long battle, prevailed. Dart Valley trains can start only at Buckfastleigh; furthermore, they have to stop short of Totnes, for to reach the BR station they would have to run for a short distance over the main line, which British Rail, understandably, does not permit.

Topped and tailed, the Dart Valley Railway has been treated harshly by authority. As I write the company is negotiating with British Rail with a view to taking over the Paignton to Kingswear branch. In this it has the support of Devon County Council and Torquay Borough Council, and larger stations would make the Kingswear line a better proposition for large numbers of passengers than the present line with its charming but small country stations. Should negotiations be successful, the railway company would have to decide whether to move lock, stock and barrel, or to run both lines.

Supporting The Dart Valley Light Railway Ltd. is the Dart Valley Railway Association. This does not consider itself a preservation society: its principal aims are to bring together persons whose interests coincide with DVLR Ltd., that is to say, to perpetuate and operate a branch-line railway representing all that was best in Great Western practice; to provide assistance, financial and otherwise, to the railway; and to invest in DVLR Ltd.

Members of the association work voluntarily on the railway. To work without pay for a company of which one of the objects is making a profit for shareholders seems to me incongruous. However, to those who do so, helping to restore and run the only GW-style branch line is its own adequate reward. This is particularly so at a time when the future of the line is in doubt and profits seem remote. In any event, the association is itself a large shareholder in the company.

Despite the authentic appearance of the railway, the people running it live in the present. They are not preserving the Great Western Railway, but running the Dart Valley Railway, on which GW practices prevail. For example, liveries of locomotives and coaches are very close to those of the GWR, but those vehicles built since nationalization, even to GWR designs, are lettered *Dart Valley* or *DVR* in Great Western style. Those which actually once belonged to the GWR do bear its name or insignia.

In 1971, trains ran from the beginning of April to the end of October, with from two to seven return journeys daily taking 50 minutes each. The peak period is from mid-July to mid-September. Buckfastleigh station has a large car park and is accessible also by bus from Newton Abbot, Totnes, Paignton, Exeter and Plymouth. It has buffet and bookstall. Passengers join and leave trains either at Buckfastleigh or the intermediate station of Staverton Bridge, 3¾ miles down the line; at Totnes Riverside (6½ miles) a new station is planned but until it is complete passengers are unable to get on or off trains. A run-round loop has already been installed. Return fare from Buckfastleigh to Totnes was 40p.

During 1971 another new loop was installed, at Staverton, to enable trains to pass one another. This will make a half-hourly train service possible and reduce overcrowding. This loop is the first section of a preserved line to be fully equipped with track circuits: that is, the rails themselves are incorporated into low-voltage electric circuits, so that trains indicate their positions to the signalman by illuminating parts of a track diagram in his signal box. At Staverton this is at the far end of the station adjacent to a level crossing. Points are electrically operated and locked. Most of the equipment was installed professionally.

The route of the railway is most pleasant: it closely follows the rocky, peaty, River Dart along its narrow, winding and well-wooded valley. At a quiet and attractive spot called Woodville, near Totnes, it was once the custom to stable the royal train overnight when their majesties were visiting the West. Now on certain evenings champagne specials pause here while a five-course dinner is served. For £5·00 passengers get a ride on the railway, dinner and as much champagne as they like. The train is chartered by the caterers.

Special trains run from many places on British Rail to Totnes and thence over the DVR to Buckfastleigh. Though composed of BR coaches they are hauled over the Dart Valley by steam locomotives. In 1971, more than a dozen such trains carried a total of 6,230 passengers. BR (Western Region) would have liked more trains still but the DVR's resources were fully extended in high summer carrying its own crowds.

School parties from Devon and Cornwall make educational visits to the railway. They get a ride on a train, a lecture on how railway and steam locomotive work, and a visit to Buckfastleigh signal-box.

The line is easily graded. Apart from a short length of 1 in 50 at the approach to Buckfastleigh, there is nothing between that station and Totnes steeper than 1 in 110.

The railway was built by the Buckfastleigh, Totnes and South Devon Railway, opened in 1872 and worked by the South Devon Railway. In 1878 it was absorbed by the Great Western. It had been built to the GWR broad gauge of 7 ft. 0¼ in. and was converted to standard gauge over a weekend in May 1892.

Sometime in its history the branch train—or possibly the engine —gained the nickname *Bulliver*. Local research into the origin of this name seems to achieve only the response: 'Us 'as allus called 'er that.'

A glance at a map shows that once motor road vehicles became practicable, the railway suffered from the disadvantage that Ashburton travellers going east could cut off two sides of a triangle and save themselves a couple of hours by taking car, bus or taxi to Newton Abbot station. Passenger trains on the branch, which had become part of British Railways, Western Region, were withdrawn on 3 November 1958, and on 10 September 1962 it was closed for goods trains also.

Moves towards reopening started almost immediately, but it was not until 18 June 1965 that The Dart Valley Light Railway Ltd. was incorporated. The first directors included Devon civil engineer R. J. S. Saunders, through whom the railway was formed, and P. B. Whitehouse and P. J. Garland of Birmingham, both long-serving Talyllyn men. Later additions to the board included A. F. Pegler, of Festiniog and Flying Scotsman, and railway publisher Ian Allan. Some of these no longer serve. The first rolling stock reappeared on the line in October 1965, and work began on refurbishing track, cutting back undergrowth and restoring stations. Signals had been taken down after passenger trains ceased and had to be replaced. All the signals now on the line, authentic though they look, have been erected by the new regime. The Dart Valley Railway Association was formed later than the company, on 22 October 1965.

Until the line was open, visitors—as many as 30,000 during the first nine months of 1968—paid to view locomotives and coaches.

Before this, on 24 November 1967, the Minister of Transport granted a light railway order to British Railways for the whole branch line to Ashburton. The Dart Valley Light Railway Ltd. then applied to the Minister for a transfer order. Three objections were made: all were met, and withdrawn by 17 June 1968. As the company had been advised by the Ministry of Transport that the transfer order would be issued approximately seven days after withdrawal of the last objection, it anticipated opening in good time for the high season for summer visitors.

At the very last moment, according to the annual report of the company chairman, the Highways Department of the Ministry of Transport made an objection concerning the section of line beyond Buckfastleigh in the Ashburton direction. This eventually crystallized as the A38 improvement scheme.

Pending a final decision on the route of the road, a compromise was arranged between Dart Valley Railway, British Railways and the ministry. BR sold to the company the branch from Totnes as far as milepost seven at Buckfastleigh, together with Ashburton station. On the intervening section the DVLR Co. leased the land but purchased the track. Total cost of purchase was about £34,000. On 1 April 1969 a light railway transfer order was granted, but only for the section from Totnes to milepost seven. This milepost is opposite the signal-box half-way along Buckfastleigh station: the passenger platforms are on the Totnes side of it and so covered by the L.R.O., but all points leading to sidings were beyond it, on the leased land.

Grant of the transfer order enabled passenger trains at last to run. They started to do so, between Buckfastleigh and Totnes Riverside, only four days later, on 5 April. On 21 May came the formal opening ceremony. This was performed by Lord Beeching, who had been chairman of British Railways when the line closed. In his speech he deplored the fact that the prettiest railways ran through the most unproductive territory, but considered that, as a tourist attraction, the Dart Valley line was a most promising proposition.

The public enquiry into the road proposals was reported in *Bulliver*, magazine of the DVRA. It was held in June 1970 before an inspector appointed by the Minister of Transport. How pleasant if applicants for light railway orders could appoint *their* own enquiry inspectors! Counsel for the DVR stated that it did not wish to delay construction of the road nor to criticize the route. A scheme had been prepared to allow both road and railway to co-exist. Evidence in support of the railway as a tourist attraction came from Devon County Council and Ashburton Urban Council. The inspector was told that the company's scheme was likely to cost £150,000.

In his report, early in 1971, the inspector concluded that the company made out a strong case, but not sufficiently strong to cause him to recommend any variation in the proposed line of the road. So it goes ahead as planned.

At Buckfastleigh a road embankment some 30 ft. high is expected to obliterate the site of sidings where coaches have been kept, and the locomotive shed at Ashburton has been isolated. New sidings have had to be laid at Staverton to accommodate locomotives and rolling stock.

Before track was lifted, there was one sad, exciting, day when steam trains ran again between Totnes and Ashburton. This was 2 October 1971. The first train, though chartered by BR, was composed of Dart Valley stock, and on this occasion it started from Totnes main-line station. It was pleasant to see a Great Western 2-6-2T puffing along the up fast line as it ran round its train! The other two trains were excursions of BR coaches; the first of these came from Swansea and the second and final one from Paddington. Both ran non-stop from Totnes to Ashburton.

Locomotives on the DVR have been selected primarily for their suitability for the line. All belong either to DVLR Ltd. or the DVRA, mostly to the former. Some have been acquired by the company from private owners or the association in exchange for shares. There are no privately owned locomotives.

All locomotives used on passenger trains are of GWR design. The stock comprises five 0-6-0 pannier tanks of various classes, two small 0-4-2Ts of the 1400 class, two 4500 class 2-6-2Ts, Manor class 4-6-0 No. 7827 *Lydham Manor*, a Peckett 0-4-0 saddle tank from Exeter gas-works (everybody has a Peckett!) and a small diesel locomotive purchased from BR and used on works trains. Engines of the 1400 and 4500 classes worked the line in GWR and BR days. One of those then familiar was No. 4555, which returned to the line as the first locomotive to be delivered for the DVR.

Busy traffic has meant that trains are often too heavy for the small locomotives. Because of this the line's second 4500 class 2-6-2T, No. 4588, was obtained by the association in 1970 from Woodham Bros.' scrap-yard at Barry for £1,750. The purchase price, together with £310 for transport over BR, was raised by a locomotive fund. After nine years in the open in a scrap-yard she required much restoration, but the need to have her in service became urgent as 4555 was due for boiler repairs.

No. 4588 was overhauled at a cost of about £10,000 at the place she had been built—Swindon Works. Now part of British Rail Engineering Ltd., it takes on outside business. But 4588 was the first steam locomotive to be overhauled there for some ten years. Swindon was no longer able to do boiler repairs, so 4588's boiler was removed for eventual overhaul elsewhere and replaced by a spare boiler which the DVR already had in stock for 4555—the virtue of standardization. On the rest of 4588, about one-fifth of the work which was needed was due to genuine wear, and four-fifths to deterioration from exposure. To give but one example, the water tanks were so badly corroded that new ones had to be made.

Dart Valley locomotives attend open days at BR locomotive depots as far away as Plymouth and Bristol and attract much attention.

Coaches on the DVR include several GWR corridor coaches and two relatively modern BR ones, bought to carry the crowds because they were in good condition and cost no more than worn GW coaches which would have needed extensive renovation. There are two GW 'super saloons' used respectively as board room by the company and clubroom by the association. They also run in the champagne specials, along with observation car *Devon Belle*. The latter is used on ordinary DVR trains as well, and in 1971, 12,200 passengers travelled in it at a supplementary fare of 20p. It derives its name from the Pullman express in which it first ran, over the Southern Railway from Waterloo. There are five GWR style 'auto trailers'. Each of these coaches has driver's controls at one end: with a suitable locomotive coupled to the other, it makes up a short train which can be driven from either end so that the engine need not run round at termini. This method of working was used in 1969 before Totnes loop was laid.

Several goods wagons and a GWR guard's van are used on works trains.

In 1971 the DVR was worked by one engine in steam between Buckfastleigh and Totnes. Whenever busy times were anticipated, special dispensation of the D.O.E. was sought to introduce train staff and ticket working. The Buckfastleigh–Ashburton section was treated as a siding. After completion of Staverton loop, it is intended to introduce electric train staff working between Buckfastleigh and Staverton, and to use train staff and ticket between there and Totnes.

The DVLR Ltd. has a paid staff of 13, under the managing director. Staff are flexible in their jobs. In winter, engine drivers, for instance, renovate coaches and firemen work on the track. At first all locomen were paid staff, but three association volunteers have recently passed as firemen. Many other tasks are undertaken by volunteers—to comply with insurance requirements, volunteers must be association members and sign a book on arrival. Because the Dart Valley has grown big quickly it pays particular attention to training staff. Early each year training weekends are held. Special trains are assembled and trainee guards, shunters and ticket collectors are shown their tasks by experienced men and then put through their paces without any passengers to get in the way! Other jobs done by volunteers include booking clerk and signalman.

When a BR train runs on to the Dart Valley, a DVR guard joins it at Totnes and acts as pilotman to the BR guard. At Buckfastleigh, Dart Valley staff and volunteers service the BR train—that is, clean it, fill water tanks, etc.

Dart Valley association members pay an annual subscription of £2·25, get unlimited free travel on the railway and receive *Bulliver* bi-monthly. The magazine goes also to company shareholders and stockholders. The association has about 2,000 members of whom about one-third live in the West Country. From being a local organization the association has grown into a national one—it has now an active group in Scotland in addition to London, Birmingham and other areas. Trustees hold the association's property and invested funds.

Authorized capital of The Dart Valley Light Railway Ltd. was £100,000 in ordinary shares of £1·00. Of this, £51,756 had been issued by 31 December 1970. As a private company, DVLR Ltd. was limited to 50 shareholders, but, with nominees, there were about 350 investors. Size of investments ranged generally from £5·00 to £2,500. Largest shareholder was the Dart Valley Railway Association, with 3,770 shares at 31 December 1971. In 1972 The DVLR Ltd increased its capital and went public, as described in appendix A.

Apart from ordinary shares the only other class of capital is 7 per cent loan stock. A total of £5,026 has been issued, a condition being that no interest was paid in the first two years and 21 per cent in the third year. The stock is redeemable by the company after January 1975 and must be redeemed by 31 December 1990.

The cost of running the railway for a season is about £30,000. This is met from the company's income. There is no grant from the association.

Three industrial railways: Sittingbourne, Leighton Buzzard, Foxfield

THE SITTINGBOURNE AND KEMSLEY LIGHT RAILWAY

For the existence of the Sittingbourne and Kemsley Light Railway we must thank a large industrial company, a well-known railway enthusiasts' organization and, as go-between, the Association of Railway Preservation Societies.

In 1965 Bowaters (UK) Paper Co. Ltd. had an extensive time-and-motion study done of paper-making processes at its paper-mills at Sittingbourne and Kemsley, Kent. One of the recommendations that emerged was that the company's 2 ft. 6 in. gauge light railway should be replaced by road vehicles. The railway carried materials, paper and personnel between the mills and to and from Ridham Dock.

The company is part of the Bowater Organization, international paper and packaging manufacturers, and no olde worlde firm. But although the board adopted the recommendation, it was fond enough of its railway and steam locomotives to look into the possibility of preservation. The company approached *The Railway Magazine*, which arranged an introduction to Captain P. Manisty, chairman of the A.R.P.S. He in turn approached the Locomotive Club of Great Britain. The LCGB was founded in 1949 and its object is to provide facilities to encourage keen interest in railway history and operation. Although a member of the A.R.P.S. its preservation activity was then limited to a single locomotive. Chairman M. Burton, himself a Kent resident, jumped at the opportunity offered by Bowaters.

After negotiations it was agreed that when Bowaters ceased to use the railway they would lease the section, almost two miles long, between Sittingbourne and Kemsley to the club at a nominal annual rental, complete with locomotives, carriages, wagons and other equipment. A handsome gesture.

FOXFIELD LIGHT RAILWAY

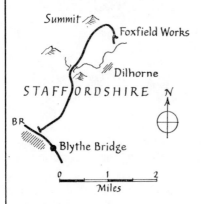

Summit

Foxfield Works

Dilhorne

STAFFORDSHIRE

N

B.R.

Blythe Bridge

0   1   2
Miles

MAP 6

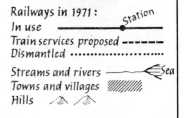
LOCHTY PRIVATE RAILWAY

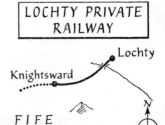

Lochty

Knightsward

FIFE

N

0   ½   1
Miles

LEIGHTON BUZZARD LIGHT AND NARROW GAUGE RAILWAYS

Sand quarry lines omitted

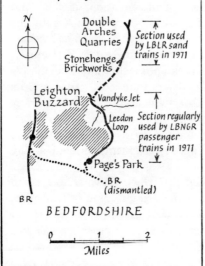

N

Double
Arches
Quarries

Section used
by LBLR sand
trains in 1971

Stonehenge
Brickworks

Leighton
Buzzard

Vandyke Jct.

Leedon
Loop

Section regularly
used by LBNGR
passenger
trains in 1971

Page's Park

B.R.
(dismantled)

B.R.

BEDFORDSHIRE

0   1   2
Miles

SITTINGBOURNE AND KEMSLEY LIGHT RAILWAY

Paper
Mill

Kemsley Down

Milton
Creek

VIADUCT

N

B.R.

Sittingbourne

KENT

0   ½   1
Miles

At a handing over ceremony on 4 October 1969 the club was granted the licence agreement for the railway. So part of the last steam narrow-gauge industrial railway in Britain was preserved and simultaneously the LCGB became the first and only established national railway society to venture into running its own railway. Because replacement road vehicles were delivered late, Bowaters unexpectedly continued to use the railway for another three weeks.

For the preserved line the title Sittingbourne and Kemsley Light Railway was adopted and to operate it the Light Railway Section of the LCGB was formed. This was reconstituted on 30 December 1971 as Sittingbourne and Kemsley Light Railway Ltd. It is limited by guarantee: its ten directors include seven appointed by the LCGB and two by Bowaters. Members are also members of the LCGB: the annual subscription is £1·00 in addition to the LCGB subscription of £1·30. Of the LCGB's 1,300 members in 1971 some 480 were also members of the Light Railway Section; of these perhaps 100 were taking an active part and about 60 were regular volunteers who ran trains, maintained line and stock and made improvements. No paid staff were employed.

During 1970 and 1971 members of the public wishing to travel on trains were admitted to day membership of the club for 30p, which entitled them to unlimited travel for one day. During 1971 the railway had 8,880 visitors. In 1972 adult return fare from Sittingbourne to Kemsley became 25p, with a day rover ticket at 30p. The only public access to the railway is at Sittingbourne, from a street called 'The Wall'. There is a car park close by and Sittingbourne British Rail and bus stations are about five minutes' walk distant. In 1971 the train service ran from 9 April to 17 October, basically at weekends but also at bank holidays, and on Thursdays in August. There were eight return journeys daily at peak holiday times and four on other days. Well-filled trains ran also on Boxing Day, when Father Christmas gave presents to children.

Sittingbourne terminus is laid out on a sharp curve on top of an embankment, where formerly were the approach sidings to the paper-mill. A stall sells refreshments and souvenirs. The line leaves the station by a long, winding, reinforced concrete viaduct and then descends to ground level; industrial surroundings give

way to open marshland. Alongside the railway runs a pipeline
carrying steam from Kemsley to Sittingbourne mill. Because of
this the SKLR has public liability insurance cover of £250,000—
an accident which damaged the pipeline would halt Sittingbourne
paper production, normally a continuous process.

The journey takes 15 minutes. The far terminus, Kemsley
Down, occupies what was formerly waste ground, close to Kemsley mill. The site was cleared and fenced by Bowaters who put
down clinker foundation to a depth of 18 inches. Bowaters also
provided track materials and buildings from those redundant
elsewhere. Light Railway Section volunteers spent their first few
months dismantling them, ahead of the scrap merchants. Now
they are laying track and re-erecting buildings. Already an office
and café building has gone up, overlooking Milton Creek. A four-
road locomotive shed and works is being added, and a museum is to
follow.

The Bowater locomotive *Leader*, a Kerr Stuart 0–4–2T, has
been purchased by a consortium of LCGB members. All the other
locomotives and rolling stock on the railway, except for some
museum exhibits, remain the property of Bowaters. There are six
more steam locomotives, and one diesel; steam locomotives in use
in 1971 were 0–4–2T *Premier* which dates from 1904 and the
earliest days of the railway, and Bagnall 0–6–2Ts *Triumph* and
Superb of 1934 and 1940 respectively. As an experiment, *Superb*
is to burn gas during 1972. All are simple, functional, well-
proportioned locomotives, handsome in their apple green livery.
Though it kept to steam, Bowaters' railway was constantly
modernized. Its five coaches were built in 1957 to replace earlier
ones. Because paper mills work 24 hours a day, the passenger
trains for personnel ran round the clock. The night trains, at 2.00
and 3.30 a.m. for instance, were I believe unique on a British
narrow-gauge railway. Many of the wagons were modern, too;
most familiar were bogie flat-wagons to carry bales of wood-pulp
(some are being converted to open-air coaches by the SLKR) but
examples of other types also are preserved.

The SKLR, though run by amateurs, has an air of professional
competence. Train staff working has been instituted and a telephone installed between the termini. To get started, the SKLR had
a loan of £1,000 from the LCGB and its members; an appeal to

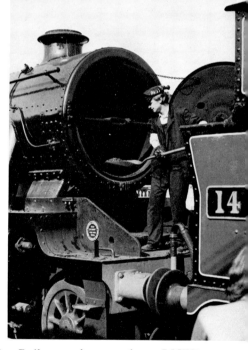

15 Men at work: *Upper*, Worth Valley Railway volunteer cleans LNER buffet car. (J. A. Cox.) *Lower left*, Bluebell Railway volunteer connects vacuum brake pipes. (Author.) *Lower Right* S V Rly, volunteer empties ashes, drawn through boiler tubes, from smokebox of 2–8–0. (Author.)

16 *upper* Talyllyn Railway staff and volunteers line up against *Dolgoch*. (J. F. Rimmer.)

lower Isle of Man Railway staff line up against *Kissack*, when she emerged from Douglas Works in 1970 fitted with a new boiler. (A. Stevenson.)

members brought in a further £400. Day membership receipts just covered cost of running the line and putting up buildings.

THE LEIGHTON BUZZARD NARROW GAUGE RAILWAY

It will by now be clear that while some locomotives on preserved railways are typical examples of once-common classes, others have been preserved because they are technically unusual. Of these one of the most curious is *Chaloner*. She is a very small o–4–oT with vertical boiler: that is, the boiler barrel is upright. At the bottom is the firebox, fed with coal through a flap in the foot-plate; mounted centrally on top of the boiler is a tall thin funnel, and on the side of the boiler toward the front of the locomotive are the cylinders, also vertical. She was built by de Winton & Co. in 1877 to work in slate quarries in North Wales. Now she runs on the two-foot gauge Leighton Buzzard Narrow Gauge Railway; and although others of her type are preserved in museums, it is only here that one of them can be appreciated to the full as she lumbers along on unsprung wheels, exuding smoke and steam (with perfect justification) from the most unexpected quarters.

Other steam locomotives at Leighton Buzzard (all, like *Chaloner*, are on loan from private owners) include *Pixie*, a diminutive Kerr Stuart o–4–o saddle tank; *The Doll*, a larger Andrew Barclay o–6–oT, and *P.C. Allen*, an o–4–oT built in Germany by Orenstein & Koppel for service at a chemical works in Spain, whence she was obtained in 1963 by that notable enthusiast for Spanish railways and sometime chairman of Imperial Chemical Industries Ltd, Sir Peter Allen. Her subsequent loan to the Leighton Buzzard railway was arranged through the Transport Trust. In late 1971 a further locomotive arrived, a Baguley o–4–oT from far-away Calcutta.

The railway on which these engines run is part of the Leighton Buzzard Light Railway. This was opened in 1919 to carry sand from quarries to the north-east of Leighton Buzzard, Bedfordshire, to exchange sidings with the London and North Western Railway 3½ miles away on the south side of the town. It was built over way-leaves without statutory powers by Leighton Buzzard

RR—K

Light Railway Ltd., which was backed by sand merchants. After brief use of two steam locomotives the LBLR adopted small internal-combustion locomotives as its sole motive power: such are still used on a short section of the north-east end of the line which continues to carry sand. In 1963 LBLR Ltd. became a wholly owned subsidiary of its principal user, sand merchant Joseph Arnold and Sons Ltd.

In 1967 the Iron Horse Preservation Society reached agreement with Arnold that it should run a passenger train service over the line at weekends. The society had been formed the previous year to display American-style steam locomotives and operate a railway based on American practice. After preparations it ran its first train in March 1968. At its annual meeting on 20 September 1969 the society decided to drop the American image and changed its name to Leighton Buzzard Narrow Gauge Railway Society. This society, according to its constitution, is non-profit-making and has two principal objects: to run a narrow-gauge light railway service along the permanent way of the LBLR, together with acquisition and restoration of locomotives and rolling stock; and establishment on the railway of a museum showing development of quarry and sand industries and the part played by narrow-gauge railways.

The society's use of the line has increased by stages as use by sand merchants declined. In 1971 it had exclusive use of the line from Page's Park, at the south end, for $2\frac{1}{4}$ miles to Stonehenge Brickworks. In return it maintains this section, pays to Leighton Buzzard Light Railway Ltd. sufficient rent to meet rates and rent due to ground landlords, and indemnifies the company against claims resulting from accidents. Apart from insurance policies the society does not yet limit liability of members: the possibility of incorporating a company is bound up with the future of LBLR Ltd. and in particular its future in 1979 when way-leaves expire. The society committee includes a planning officer who concerns himself with such things. Pending developments, two trustees hold the society's rolling stock and other property.

Page's Park station of the Leighton Buzzard Narrow Gauge Railway is to be found up a short sandy pathway which leads off Billington Road. There is a car park close to the entrance to the pathway. The station faces a leafy park of the same name; behind it is a sand quarry. The sidings, platform and buildings are the work of the society—the two road locomotive shed and stores were built largely from salvaged materials, and there are bookstall and refreshment kiosk.

Trains in 1971 ran on Sundays from 28 March to 31 October, on Saturdays for a more limited period and on bank holidays, the first train each operating day leaving Page's Park at 14.00. The following winter, trains ran on the first Sunday in each month, and on 27 December Father Christmas visited the railway to *drive P.C. Allen*. Normal destination of trains is Leedon loop, just over one mile from Page's Park; cost of a journey there and back was 15p. Occasional trains ran as far as Vandyke Junction, 1¾ miles, and specials sometimes travel the whole route. Between Page's Park and Vandyke Junction the line swings in a semi-circle round the edge of Leighton Buzzard, with housing estates on one side and fields on the other, interspersed with occasional factories which use sand as a raw material, formerly supplied by the railway.

There are four coaches, with bodies built by the society on the underframes of bogie wagons. Early versions were open-air, but recent coaches are roofed in and future coaches will be. Small brake-vans, with passenger accommodation, have been built on the weighty chassis of old diesel locomotives. Goods vehicles include a weed-killer tank wagon, flat wagons to carry sleepers and rails, and a small mobile crane. There are several diesel locomotives in addition to the steam locomotives. Society members have re-sleepered about half a mile of track using second-hand BR sleepers cut into halves.

Visitors to the railway increased from 5,891 in 1969 to 6,786 in 1970 and 9,809 in the summer of 1971. Sunday is busier than Saturday, when people go shopping, and the ends of the summer season are busier than July and August, when people are away on holiday. The railway is operated by train staff and card tickets under the operating manager, one of eight senior members on a roster for the job. Marley's loop, mid-way between Page's Park and Leedon loop, is sometimes used for trains to cross. The railway is run and maintained entirely by volunteers; of the society's membership of 190, about 30 take an active part. Most of these live in the home counties north of London. Members pay an annual subscription of £2·00.

THE FOXFIELD LIGHT RAILWAY

Despite the proximity of the Potteries, the region a few miles to the east of Stoke-on-Trent, Staffordshire, is rural, hilly and attractive. As you admire the view from a hill near the village of Dilhorne the only blemish is a small colliery and its buildings. They rapidly redeem themselves, however, when from them arise white plumes of steam and puffs of smoke to indicate the presence of steam locomotives. The colliery is now Foxfield Works, head-quarters of the Foxfield Light Railway.

The railway, which is standard gauge and 3⅜ miles long, was built in 1893 by the owners of the colliery to link it with the main railway system. It made a junction with the North Staffordshire Railway about 400 yards west of Blythe Bridge station. Until August 1965 the railway fulfilled its original purpose; then the colliery was closed and locomotives used on the railway were dispersed.

Colliery and railway were purchased by Tean Minerals Ltd. which now processes minerals in the colliery buildings and considered using the railway to receive stone. This plan did not materialize and the connection with the main line has now been removed. But the directors of Tean Minerals are sympathetic towards railway preservation and as a result the Foxfield Light Railway Society was formed in 1966. In 1971 it was incorporated as a guarantee company, Foxfield Light Railway Society Ltd., at the recommendation of the A.R.P.S.

The society's main object is to operate steam locomotives over the Foxfield line at weekends and bank holidays by permission of the owner. Though trains ran originally for the enjoyment of members, in order to provide revenue passenger trains now run on certain days. During the summer of 1971 these were the second Sunday in each month. Visitors wishing to travel became day members for 25p. During 1970 almost 1,000 visitors did so and in 1971 the number rose to 1,900. They came from as far afield as London and Yorkshire as well as nearby towns.

On operating days the first train leaves Foxfield at 2 p.m., with further departures at about 40 minute intervals. Some trains traverse the whole line to Blythe Bridge but others are short workings. Foxfield Works is best reached from the South via the A50 road, turning northwards off it at Blythe Bridge and passing through Dilhorne.

All nine steam locomotives on the line are of industrial origin and all are saddle tanks, some having 0–4–0 wheel arrangement and some 0–6–0. The 0–4–0ST *Henry Cort*, built by Peckett in 1903, belongs to the society; the remainder are privately owned. Dates of building range from 1895 to 1947. The society also owns a small Simplex diesel locomotive and an LMS bogie corridor coach. Other rolling stock includes a steam crane and four LMS bogie vans which once carried scenery for touring theatrical companies. One of these has had openings made in its sides and ends and is pressed into service at busy times to carry passengers, as also is a four-wheeled wagon which has been restored to the livery of private owner T. Bolton and Sons Ltd. There are two four-wheeled goods vans and a Midland Railway style brake-van.

Foxfield Works has a triangular track layout and trains leave from a short platform built near the apex of the triangle. The line leaves the works on a gradient as steep as 1 in 22 for a few hundred feet which eases to approximately 1 in 30 for half a mile. It describes a semi-circle as it climbs, giving panoramic views towards hills to the north-east, until it reaches the summit in a small wood. Here are two short sidings: formerly loaded wagons of coal were brought up five at a time and then assembled into a train for the remainder of the journey to Blythe Bridge. The route is now downhill all the way, through the countryside. Only for the final few hundred yards does a built-up area appear in the distance.

A senior member acts as controller each operating day. The line is divided into two sections, from Foxfield to Summit and Summit to Blythe Bridge, with train staffs for each. Over the first section trains generally run with an engine at each end—the lower engine banks on the way up and the top engine provides additional braking power on the way down. Trains cross at Summit and the banking engine of the train which has just come up transfers itself to the rear of the train about to descend. At Blythe Bridge there are sidings, and a run-round loop is being laid; until it is ready the diesel is stationed there on operating days to shunt the train so that its steam locomotive may be transferred from one end to the other. Short workings from Foxfield as far as Summit only run with one engine, at the downhill end.

The society has the use of the works' small locomotive shed with pit, but much maintenance has to be done in the open. Maintenance goes on every weekend. About 20 of the society's 100 members form a hard core of volunteers and most of these live within a ten-mile radius of the railway. They could do with more assistance for, in my observation, weeds and undergrowth seem to be encroaching over basically sound permanent way, despite endeavours to keep them in check. The annual subscription is £2·00. There are no paid staff. Agreement with Tean Minerals Ltd. has so far been informal, though the society pays part of the rates on the line. A formal lease of the line, or even purchase, is a possibility.

13   The Lochty Private Railway

The largest locomotive mentioned in this book runs on the shortest railway. She is A4 class 4-6-2 No. 60009 *Union of South Africa*, which weighs 103 tons and runs on the Lochty Private Railway which is about 1½ miles long. She does so as a result of British Rail's ban on operation of steam locomotives over its lines.

The Lochty railway is the only preserved steam railway in Scotland. Its station at Lochty is near St. Andrews, Fife, on road B940 with a bus service past the gate and signposts erected by the Automobile Association. Trains run on the afternoons of Sundays and public holidays in June, July and August, with frequent departures from Lochty station. Return fare to Knightsward, the far terminus, was 20p in 1971.

Preservation of *Union of South Africa* and the existence of the Lochty Private Railway are due to one man, John B. Cameron. When steam was going out on British Railways, he decided to attempt to preserve one of the A4 class 4-6-2s. These streamlined locomotives were built by the LNER and from the late thirties until the early sixties they hauled the principal expresses over the East Coast Route from King's Cross to Leeds, Newcastle, Edinburgh and Aberdeen. Object of streamlining was to reduce air resistance at speed; in practice the publicity it gained was probably as important.

With friends at all levels on the Scottish Region of BR, J. B. Cameron learned that the A4 in best condition was *Union of South Africa*, one of several engines in the class named after dominions. Although she had been withdrawn early with a minor defect, which often happened in the last days of steam, she was basically sound and had been the last main-line steam locomotive to be overhauled at BR's Doncaster Works, in 1963. She was interesting, too, from the historic point of view. She had regularly been rostered to haul the famous *Coronation* express when it was introduced in 1937. She had frequently hauled the royal train. In

1965 she hauled the last express out of King's Cross for which a
steam locomotive was rostered.

The following year J. B. Cameron agreed to buy her for about
£3,000. Because her own tender was defective, she was accom-
panied by the tender from another A4, No. 60004. To own *Union
of South Africa*, Cameron formed a small share company with
friends; he and his wife are directors. The company later became
the Lochty Private Railway Co. Ltd.

At first *Union of South Africa*, though privately owned, was
kept on BR metals. At Easter 1967 she successfully hauled over
part of its route a Grand Scottish Tour train organized by British
Rail. The train was so popular that 18 coaches were needed to
accommodate all the passengers and a pilot engine had to be
added. This excursion might have been the first of many. Then
BR banned steam locomotives.

J. B. Cameron is a farmer, in a big way of business, with several
farms. One of these, then recently purchased, is Lochty Farm.
Across it ran the last mile and a half of the East Fife Central
Railway, which had been closed by BR 18 months earlier. J. B.
Cameron was able to purchase this. As a place to run *Union
of South Africa* it had good qualifications. It was bordered by his
own farmland and had no public road crossings. No statutory
authority had to be obtained. The track was substantial enough to
carry an A4 at low speeds. Some of it, however, had been lifted;
additional track needed was purchased from a colliery. A brick and
corrugated iron shed was built, so that the locomotive would be
safe under lock and key and sheltered from wind and rain. *Union
of South Africa* was delivered to Lochty by road, for the private
railway was already cut off from BR.

The Lochty Private Railway was inaugurated on 14 June 1967.
The assistant general manager of BR's Scottish Region unveiled
a plaque on the locomotive and 100 guests were entertained. That
summer *Union of South Africa* ran up and down as a light engine.
She attracted crowds large enough for J. B. Cameron to decide to
obtain rolling stock and carry passengers. He purchased an
appropriate vehicle—one of the observation cars built for the
Coronation express hauled by *Union of South Africa* thirty years
before.

In it some 3,000 passengers were carried in 1968. Two years

later the number had increased so much that a second coach was obtained, for the 1971 season. That year the number of passengers carried rose to around 6,000, even though the railway only ran on about 14 afternoons during the year. Operation shows a small surplus, put towards maintenance and depreciation.

Neither end of the line has a loop, so trains run forwards from Lochty to Knightsward and are propelled on the return journey. Speeds are not fast—about 20 m.p.h. Signals and small signal-boxes have been erected at each station. At Lochty station the original platform survives; at Knightsward, where there was once a halt, now dismantled, a new small platform has been built.

There are no paid staff—all helpers are volunteers. Some are steam-experienced men from BR, some are members of the Thornton Railway Club. An operating Sunday sees about a dozen at work, including foot-platemen, guard, station staff, and track maintenance men. Maintenance of *Union of South Africa* has so far been no great problem, for she was overhauled before leaving BR and now does no hard work. She is being kept in her final, familiar, British Railways livery. Another locomotive, of industrial type, has been purchased and is expected on the Lochty railway soon.

Late News. Following the announcement that in 1973 steam locomotives would be allowed to make a limited number of runs over British Rail between Dundee and Dunfermline, negotiations started for 60009 to return to the tracks of BR. Should they be successful, the Lochty Private Railway may still continue to operate, though with a smaller locomotive.

14 Plans and prosperity: Some schemes for more preserved steam railways

The previous 12 chapters describe all railways within the definitions at the beginning of chapter one—that is, British preserved steam railways operated with voluntary support in 1971. Two other railways which almost qualified are next described.

The Chasewater Light Railway's passenger trains ran on 1971 summer Sundays over half a mile of track but were powered by vintage diesel locomotives dating from the 1920s. The full length of the line is two miles and it is planned to run along all of it when track has been cleared and an embankment strengthened— probably by 1973. There are already steam locomotives on the railway, and though these had not run regularly, it was hoped to improve the position in 1972.

The Chasewater Light Railway Co. Ltd. is controlled by the Railway Preservation Society. Its shareholders are RPS members and others. The line's depot is at Brownhills, Staffordshire, and the railway is run under the auspices of Aldridge–Brownhills council. The entrance to the depot is in Pool Road, itself a turning off the A5 main road, and the line runs close to Chasewater, a canal reservoir which now sees sailing and power-boat races, water skiing and so forth.

The railway is standard gauge and gave access to collieries before it was closed in 1960. It then lay derelict until 1965 when it was acquired under a long-term lease from the National Coal Board by the Railway Preservation Society. It is now isolated from the main railway system. The company was formed to operate trains in close liaison with the society.

The society itself dates from 1959 and initially preserved railway equipment at another location. The working line came later. The society was formed as the West Midland District of the (national) Railway Preservation Society. This evolved into the more loose-knit Association of Railway Preservation Societies and its districts became autonomous societies, early A.R.P.S. members.

The society owns six steam locomotives, of which five are industrial saddle tanks built between 1882 and 1911; the sixth is 0–6–0T *Cannock Wood*, built by the LBSCR in 1877 and sold to a colliery in 1926. Coaches include an LNWR travelling post office (i.e. postal sorting van) of 1909, and a six-wheeled Maryport and Carlisle Railway coach which is used to carry passengers. The railway is an entirely voluntary organization and could do with more than the 120 members that the society has. Adult annual subscription is £1·50.

The Romney Hythe and Dymchurch Light Railway was fully active in 1971, but facing closure at the end of the season. This 15 in. gauge line with its nine miniature express locomotives runs from Hythe, Kent, for 14 miles to Dungeness. It is unique and has often been described in print. The railway was a dream fulfilled for Captain J. E. P. Howey who financed and built it in 1926 and managed it himself until his death in 1963. It subsequently passed to local business people who endeavoured to run it commercially. To cater for people interested in the railway the RHDR Association was formed: it operated independently though maintaining a friendly relationship with the company, and members did some voluntary work on the railway.

The owners of the company extracted a 4 per cent annual dividend until arrears of maintenance caught up with them in 1971. They then decided to sell. The most profitable way to dispose of the railway would have been to break it up—in addition to the value of locomotives and equipment, stations occupied valuable sites. Happily the owners were prepared to sell control for £80,000 to a consortium which was formed to continue operation of the line.

The consortium, headed by W. H. McAlpine and J. B. Hollingsworth, raised the necessary cash, and more for working capital, from about 20 subscribers, partly by loans. Subscribers included two bodies representing groups of small contributors: Hythe Chamber of Commerce and the RHDR Association. Control of the railway changed hands in February 1972. The consortium formed a holding company to own shares in the statutory light railway company.

All subscribers get shares and loan stock in the holding company, but dividends and interest are not envisaged. Rather, it is intended to lean heavily on volunteer talent for the railway's continued development in the Festiniog manner. Since it carries over 300,000 passengers a year it is expected to be viable. The immediate need is to obtain sufficient revenue to overtake arrears of maintenance and secure the future of the line. One idea is property development at Hythe station, incorporating the railway.

That all possibilities in reviving a railway are far from exhausted is demonstrated by the projected North Yorkshire Moors Railway. Its organizing body expects to be a charity, and has both extensive local authority backing and the largest membership of individuals of any preserved railway, open or not.

The railway which is the object of the scheme is standard gauge and starts at a junction with BR's Whitby to Middlesbrough line at Grosmont, Yorkshire. It is hoped to reopen it either to Ellerbeck (six miles) or possibly as far as Pickering (18 miles). The line dates from the 1830s and runs through the North York Moors National Park. Formalities of setting up the North York Moors Historical Railway Charitable Trust Ltd. are being finalized at the time of writing. It is to be an education charity, to promote preservation of the railway for the public, preserve its character and amenities, and improve access to the national park. It is also to give the public the opportunity to observe the railway and enable young persons to engage in creative and educational leisure activities.

Five local authorities support the scheme, being conscious of the railway's potential for tourism and employment. One of them, North Riding County Council, is to provide financial assistance for purchase of the line from British Rail. Agreement has been reached for purchase of land and track as far as Ellerbeck, together with the land only from there to Pickering, for £42,500. Negotiations continue for the track from Ellerbeck to Pickering— estimated cost is £60,000. A light railway order has been made to British Rail and a transfer order is expected.

Pending this, railway weekends are held during which trains are run, composed of independently owned stock housed on the line. Only members may travel, but 'instant membership' (for one year) is available on the spot. From this largely springs record membership—over 6,000. There is also important support from local people who consider the railway is needed as a public service, especially in winter when roads are blocked by snow. The railway is committed to offering such a service.

Although in 1971 no preserved railways were operated by public companies set up for preservation, two such companies had been formed in connection with proposals for preserved railways. The first of these lines is the North Norfolk Railway. The origin of this scheme goes back to 1959 when the Midland and Great Northern Joint Railway Society was formed to preserve a section of the closed MGNJ Railway in Norfolk. A private company, Central Norfolk Enterprises Ltd., was incorporated in 1963 to take over negotiations, with the society as a shareholder.

The scheme has been beset by difficulties arising from personality problems and differences of opinion. I doubt if any preserved railway has been entirely free from upsets on this score, but harmony is more common and the MGNJ scheme has had more than its fair share of trouble. Things reached a nadir about 1968, when the A.R.P.S., of which the society was a member, was appointed arbitrator. As a result Central Norfolk Enterprises Ltd. was taken in hand by a compromise team of directors and renamed 'North Norfolk Railway Co. Ltd.' The MGNJR Society supports it. The company had obtained some rolling stock and purchased track on the section Sheringham to Weybourne, though the land beneath it remained to be bought. It also had liabilities—debts, loans, creditors—amounting to several thousand pounds; and it had about £35·00 in the kitty. Unless substantial finance could be raised quickly to set the scheme on its feet, track and rolling stock would have had to have been sold.

Finance was raised by 'going public' and offering an issue of shares for sale: 17,509 shares at £1·00 each. The law imposes strict conditions under which a company may raise money in this way. It must disclose its situation fully, including debts and liabilities, and it must make public an audited statement of assets. These it does in its prospectus. And if it has either not commenced business, or has recently been converted from private to public, or has not previously published a prospectus, it must declare the minimum amount needed for objects set out (£11,700 in the North Norfolk instance). If this is not subscribed within 40 days all funds raised must be refunded.

Preparing any prospectus is complex and expensive. North Norfolk Railway's prospectus took eight months to prepare and cost over £1,200 including printing. There was no money left over for advertising, though the unusual nature of the prospectus, in which the directors could not forecast when dividends might be paid, got it press mention from the *Financial Times* to the *Morning Star*. The prospectus was published in November 1969; by the end of the 40 days, £14,000 had been raised—probably more money than any other railway preservation appeal had ever raised so quickly. After a year the figure had grown to £15,500.

The company now has about 550 shareholders with an average holding around £25·00. In addition to these, the MGNJR Society has 4,265 shares. Further finance is needed to get the railway over the hump of starting to operate, and another issue of shares is planned, as forecast in the first prospectus. Payment for these shares will be linked to grant of light railway orders, for the first of which application has been made.

The other public company is the Yorkshire Dales Railway Co. Ltd. This project began in 1968 with formation of the Embsay and Grassington Railway Preservation Society. It aimed to operate the branch from Grassington to the junction at Embsay, on the Skipton to Ilkeley line, as a preserved railway. Since part of the Grassington branch was still in use for mineral traffic and not for sale, the society diverted its attention to Embsay station, close to the junction but on the line to Ilkeley which was closed. On this 18-acre site has been established the Embsay Steam Centre and Working Transport Museum.

The society changed its name in 1970 to Yorkshire Dales Railway Society and later that year the limited company was formed as a private company to handle the society's business affairs. In April

1971 it went public with an issue of 36,000 ordinary shares of 25p each. As expected the issue was not fully subscribed but it raised useful capital. The company, with the support of the society and a galaxy of vice-presidents, is now building up Embsay centre by business-like methods. It boasts, for instance, the only full-time model railway shop on a preserved railway location. Long-term aim remains operation of the Grassington branch complete, perhaps, with freight traffic.

There are many more projects for preserved railways. To produce a complete description of all of them at a given time would be almost impossible. Those I have mentioned had features not duplicated on lines already operating; I hope protagonists of all the others will excuse their omission.

Nor, unfortunately, does space permit details of overseas lines. Preserved steam railways administered on the British pattern have spread to France, Belgium, Germany, Switzerland, Denmark, Sweden, Australia and probably other countries also. In North America the British idea of a voluntary preservation society does not seem to have caught on, but there are many railway museums and steam tourist lines.

To propose a preserved railway is one thing; to succeed in reviving it and operating a scheduled train service is quite another. Many schemes have fallen by the wayside. Some that spring to mind are those for the Westerham Branch, the Waverley Route from Edinburgh to Carlisle, the Sandy and Potton line, the Longmoor Military Railway and the Hayling Island Branch. It would be instructive to dissect the causes of failure, which include conflict with road improvements, opposition by local residents, lack of finance, and too much enthusiasm allied with too little practical knowledge. But full details are hard to come by.

Although I have attempted to describe revived railways as fully as possible, there are aspects of which lack of space has prevented detailed mention. Such are time-tabling and diagramming of trains, and tickets and collection of fares, both complex and fascinating subjects. I must also pay tribute to the large amount of voluntary work done by society and association members away from the railway they support, in the forms of practical homework, publicity, and administration such as receiving subscriptions, keeping membership records and editing magazines.

It is no coincidence that the period during which steam railways have revived has been one of increasing prosperity generally. Prosperity has provided people with cars and so caused closure of branch-line railways: at the same time it has provided people with enough leisure and funds to revive railways voluntarily, using their cars to reach them.

Appendix A
Recent Developments

Preserved steam railways are developing so quickly that there have inevitably been events of importance during the interval between completing the manuscript of this book and correcting the proofs. These events are here described:—

TALYLLYN RAILWAY

Celebration of the 21st anniversary of the Talyllyn Railway Preservation Society took place on 12 May 1972 with special trains. But it was a muted celebration, for by sad coincidence the late Edward Thomas had died a few days previously, and his funeral was on the same day.

FESTINIOG RAILWAY

The company received a total in round figures of £106,700 from the Central Electricity Generating Board in settlement of its compensation claim. This will enable it to have some of the work on the Llyn Ystradau Deviation done by contract—such as boring the tunnel. The prototype of a new class of bogie coach, with aluminium body and electric storage heaters, has gone into service. *Porthmadog*, the Welsh spelling for *Portmadoc*, has come into general use.

WELSHPOOL AND LLANFAIR LIGHT RAILWAY

The section from Castle Caereinion to Sylfaen was reopened as planned on 15 July 1972.

ISLE OF MAN RAILWAY

The Isle of Man Railway Company came back into direct rail operation early in 1972. This was very much a rescue operation, when negotiations between Lord Ailsa and the Isle of Man Tourist Board broke down after the board had widely publicized a steam train service for the summer. By mutual agreement the railway company re-obtained possession of the railway system

from Lord Ailsa on 1 March 1972. It then leased the Port Erin
line and most of Douglas station to the tourist board, as planned;
but by agreement with the board, the line is operated by the
IOMR Co. itself.

From 5 June to 15 September four trains ran daily in each
direction between Douglas and Port Erin, on Mondays to Fridays
only. The title of the operation reverted to *Isle of Man Railway*.
The railway company receives from the tourist board the rent
for the line (£9,000 a year) irrespective of financial results, plus
a subsidy of up to £12,000 a year for proved operating losses. For
1973 a similar train service is planned, with an additional train
service in late May and early June for schools traffic from England. Under present arrangements the company is expected to
run the Port Erin line until the end of the 1974 season; discussions
have already started regarding the position subsequently. As for
the lines to Peel and Ramsey, unused since 1968, the company is
preparing to sell them off—a big job because a multitude of
deeds exists.

Her Majesty the Queen and members of the royal family
travelled on the IOMR from Castletown to Douglas on 2 August
1972. Locomotive *Kissack* hauled a four-coach train including
saloon No. F36, built in 1905, in which the royal party travelled.

The operating centenary of the railway company was due
to be celebrated on 1 July 1973 with special commemorative
trains.

The railway company now gets on well with the Isle of Man
Steam Railway Supporters' Association after a period when relations were rather strained. Its four directors are all association
members, and on occasion the association chairman meets the
company board to discuss co-operation. Volunteers continue to
do good work on the railway as ticket clerks and collectors, and
supplementary guards-brakesmen. But the railway needs persons
prepared to take picks, shovels and sickles in their hands: and the
company is prepared to make ex gratia payments to men with com-
mitments who are prepared to do essential track and lineside work.

SEVERN VALLEY RAILWAY

The issue of shares in Severn Valley Railway (Holdings) Ltd,
was over-subscribed: on 12 April 1972, 58,000 shares of £1·00

each were offered and £82,690 was received. Of the applicants for shares, 1,097 were members of the guarantee company, and these received the numbers of shares for which they had applied. The remaining shares were distributed among the other applicants, and £24,690 had to be returned.

In view of this the directors immediately made the planned rights issue. On 14 July 1972, 50,000 shares of £1·00 each were offered to ordinary shareholders in the proportion of one new share for every two shares already allotted; this had raised £28,079 by 25 August, and the offer remained open for a time.

A total of 1,500 shares was taken up by the Severn Valley Railway Association. This had been formed in July 1971 when plans envisaged winding up the guarantee company after formation of the share company, and its principal object was to safeguard the interests of members of the SVR Co. Ltd. (by guarantee). When it was decided that this company would continue after all, it appeared to me that the association would, after a brief life, be wound up—hence no mention of it in chapter ten. But as I write it too continues in existence, acting as a sort of watchdog.

The British Railways Board applied for an L.R.O. for the southern section of the Severn Valley line on 16 June 1972, in anticipation of a further order to transfer it to SVR (Holdings) Ltd. Current plans envisage that the holdings company will own the whole line and the guarantee company will operate it.

DART VALLEY RAILWAY

The Dart Valley Light Railway Ltd. purchased the Paignton to Kingswear line in 1972 from British Railways for a price in excess of £200,000. A light railway order for the line was made to BR on 13 July 1972 and a transfer order followed on 8 November. Trains continued to run without interruption, four trains each way daily being run during the winter by the DVR, with the aid of a subsidy from Devon County Council, to carry school children and others. The great advantage of taking over a railway without interruption was that things were in good condition, maintained to passenger-carrying standards. There was no interval of closure and dereliction.

The line actually purchased by the DVR extends from Kingswear for six miles to Goodrington Sands Halt; there is an intermediate station at Churston and a few hundred yards of the former branch from that station to Brixham are included. From Goodrington Sands, DVR trains exercise running powers over BR for ¾ mile into Paignton station.

Prior to the purchase, The Dart Valley Light Railway Ltd. increased its authorized capital to £350,000 and went public. It offered no less than 250,000 ordinary shares of £1·00 each to the public on 2 October 1972 and this large issue was successful: as I write the minimum figure of £190,000 has been subscribed and shares continue to sell.

The company will go on operating its Totnes to Buckfastleigh line also, and privately owned locomotives may be introduced on both lines.

CHASEWATER LIGHT RAILWAY

Steam-hauled passenger trains commenced during the summer of 1972.

LAKESIDE AND HAVERTHWAITE RAILWAY

On 13 October 1972 an L.R.O. was made to the British Railways Board for the Haverthwaite to Lakeside section of its closed branch line from Plumpton Junction, near Ulverston, Lancs, to Lakeside, which is at the south end of Windermere lake. A further order was anticipated to transfer this 3-mile-long standard-gauge line to the Lakeside and Haverthwaite Railway Co. Ltd. which intends, with the support of the Lakeside Railway Society, to operate it with steam trains.

If, as is hoped, the transfer order is made in February 1973, the train service will probably be running before this is published. An hourly service is proposed, running in connection with BR's motor vessel service on the lake. At Lakeside, the station is adjacent to the quay; and at Haverthwaite, the station is beside the A590 main road.

Locomotives and rolling stock have already been delivered (they include a class 5MT 4-6-0 and two class 4MT 2-6-4Ts, all of LMS design, and bogie coaches of early BR standard types), volunteers have trained on the Worth Valley Railway, and test trains between Haverthwaite and Lakeside have run.

Appendix B
Fundamentals of steam locomotives and railways

Although British Rail ceased to use steam locomotives in 1968 (with the tiny exception of their Vale of Rheidol narrow-gauge line), the appearance of a steam locomotive must surely still be familiar. Usually it consists of a large, long, more or less cylindrical *thing* with a chimney at one end, a cab with foot-plate for driver and fireman at the other and a lot of wheels underneath. The cylindrical *thing* comprises, from front to back, sections called smoke-box, boiler and firebox. In the firebox burns the fire, usually of coal, to heat water in the boiler and make steam, under pressure. Steam passes to cylinders, low down at the front of the locomotive, in which it pushes pistons to and fro; the pistons are connected by rods to the wheels to make them go round. Simple.

To go into a little more detail: the fire burns fiercely, in the inner firebox; between it and the outer firebox is a space for water. From the fire, burning gases and smoke pass through the boiler in tubes to the smokebox, and thence to the chimney. This arrangement of inner and outer firebox and boiler tubes enables a large enough heated surface to be in contact with the water to produce adequate steam. Pressure of steam ranges from about 80 to about 250 lb. per sq. in., according to locomotive. On top of the boiler are spring-loaded safety valves. When steam pressure becomes too high, they open automatically to release excess steam with a spectacular roar. Periodically, to check that boilers are safe, and satisfy the insurance company's boiler inspector, they are given a hydraulic test: water is pumped into them to a pressure perhaps half as high again as the normal working pressure.

Steam from the boiler passes first through a regulator valve, opened by the driver according to the speed at which he wishes the train to travel, and then to further valves which admit it to and release it from the cylinders. These valves are operated by valve gear, that is rods and links driven from wheels or axles, but they are adjusted by the driver so that the engine goes forwards or back-wards. Exhaust steam is released from cylinders after each piston-stroke, and passes through the smokebox and out of the chimney—hence the puffing noise. *En route* it gathers up smoke from the fire: the harder the engine works, the more exhaust steam there is to draw the fire up and make more steam still. A steam whistle is sounded by the driver to warn of the train's presence, or, when stationary, that it is about to move.

Backbone of a locomotive is the frames; on them are mounted the other components and below them the wheels. Since there is little adhesion between steel wheel and steel rail (wheels tend to 'slip' or spin) all steam locomotives in use on preserved railways have at least four driving wheels—two driven from the pistons by connecting rods and the others linked to them by coupling rods. Some locomotives have six, eight or more driving wheels. Some, too, have small carrying wheels before or behind the driving wheels. These spread the weight of the locomotive, and, when arranged to swivel, ease its passage round curves. A handy form of shorthand describes locomotives' wheel arrangements: for example, 4-6-2, four leading carrying wheels followed by six driving wheels followed in turn by two trailing wheels; 2-4-0, two leading wheels followed by four driving wheels only; 0-6-0, six driving wheels only. This indicates a locomotive's length and size. It also indicates, to those in the know, its purpose—which might be hauling passenger or freight trains, or shunting, or 'mixed traffic'; that is to say, hauling either passengers or freight accord-ing to demand. Various wheel arrangements suit various tasks.

Coal and water supplies are carried on a tender coupled immedi-ately behind the locomotive; or, on a tank engine, in bunker and tanks on the locomotive itself. Since capacity of these is small, tank engines were for short runs. They were often preferred for branch lines. The letter T added to the wheel arrangement, as in 0-4-0T, indicates a tank engine. Most common position for water tanks is one each side of the boiler, i.e. a side tank engine. There are also tanks mounted over the boiler (saddle tank-'ST'), slung one each side of the boiler (pannier tank-'PT'), or hidden between the frames (well tank-'WT'). Each of these variations gives a locomotive a distinct appearance.

By motor-car standards, steam locomotives are simple, solid,

large, expensive and inefficient. Because they are simple, they
demand more skill from the driver—not so much is done automatically. They are made, principally, from steel plate up to 1½ in.
thick or more, and castings of bronze or iron. They weigh, in
round figures, between 10 and 100 tons. The cost of a new full-
size locomotive for a preserved railway would at the present time
be prohibitive. But they are long lived—they used to average
around 40 years, and by steady replacement of worn parts, from
bearings to boilers, they seem to last for ever. They were built in
small quantities, from ones and twos up to classes of a few hundred.
Steam locomotives have enough individuality to be given names and
spoken of, like ships, as *she*. Finally, they do not start at the press of
a button. Because a lot of water has to boil, the time from lighting
up a fire in a steam locomotive until it is ready to haul a train ranges
from one to seven hours. This time is not wasted—it is spent
cleaning, polishing, oiling and, in the process, checking that all is
in order. In the author's experience it is seldom long enough!

Behind locomotive and tender come the coaches or carriages
which make up the train. Usually each coach has eight wheels in
two four-wheeled bogies. The latter swivel to enable a long coach
to pass round sharp curves, and pivot to reduce bumps. Early
coaches had four or six wheels—some survive on preserved railways. Inside, passengers find either full-width compartments,
which fit the most people into a coach, or compartments with side
corridors and connections to adjoining coaches, or open saloons
with tables between the seats. Coach interiors reflect the taste of
the period in which they were built—Victorian, Edwardian, 1930s
or 1950s. Many preserved railways have both museum-piece
coaches run infrequently if at all, and relatively modern vehicles
acquired or built to carry holiday-making crowds. Some small
lines have open-air coaches and all have an assortment of goods
vehicles used mainly to carry materials for maintenance.

Somewhere in the train rides the guard, either in his own brake-
van or in a brake compartment in a composite coach. On many
preserved railways, passenger trains are fitted with continuous
automatic vacuum brakes. Brake blocks on each vehicle are worked
from a piston in a vertical cylinder. The cylinders are connected
by pipes to each other and to the locomotive, with flexible couplings between vehicles.

When the brakes are off, each piston is at the bottom of its cylinder. Before the train moves, a partial vacuum is created throughout cylinders and pipes. To apply brakes, air is admitted by a valve, in driver's cab or guard's brake-van, through the pipes to the undersides of the pistons: atmospheric pressure pushes them upwards.

This not only enables driver or guard to apply brakes simultaneously on each vehicle, but means that should the train split in two air enters the vacuum pipes and automatically applies brakes in both parts of the train. 'Fail-safe' principles such as this are common features of railway equipment.

Railway track provides a smooth path for trains, spreads their weight over the ground and guides them; it comprises steel rails fastened to wood or concrete sleepers which rest in stone ballast. Weight, and so strength, of rails is matched to speed and weight of trains anticipated, from 20 to 110 lb. a yard. 'Flat bottom' rail is spiked or screwed, with or without baseplates, to sleepers, and other types such as 'bullhead' are wedged by wooden or steel keys in cast iron-chairs which are screwed to the sleepers. It depends on how robust the track needs to be and how much money is available.

Railway vehicles are guided by flanges on their wheels which bear on the inside edges of the rails. The rails are held to gauge, that is kept the correct distance apart, by the sleepers which also transmit weight of trains to the ballast. This not only provides a level surface for sleepers but also enables rain water to soak away. If water does collect under sleepers, passing trains pump them up and down, which makes cavities and very quickly causes most uneven track. So lineside ditches have to be kept clear also. Rails are joined to their neighbours either by fish-plates, bolts and nuts, or by welding. *Fish*, in this sense, is derived from an early meaning of the French *ficher*—to fix.

Since steam trains combine heavy weights with relatively low power and low adhesion, gradients have to be as gentle as possible. So for much of its length a railway runs on embankments, in cuttings, through tunnels and over viaducts The standard gauge was used for most railways in Britain. Narrow-gauge railways were cheaper to build, directly in cost of materials and indirectly because they could go round sharper curves which reduced the cost of earthworks and civil engineering features in hilly districts. A few narrow-gauge lines were built where these advantages outweighed their disadvantages—slow speed and low capacity of trains, and inconvenience and cost of transferring passengers and goods at exchange stations with standard-gauge lines. A disproportionate number of preserved railways are narrow gauge— partly because slow narrow-gauge trains were worse hit by road competition than standard-gauge ones, so narrow-gauge lines closed earlier; partly because they are relatively cheap for preservation groups to restore and maintain; and partly just because small trains appeal.

Trains, big or small, are unable to pull up suddenly. For safety, railways are divided into 'block sections' and only one train at a time is allowed in each section. On single lines with loops for trains to pass one another—as were most preserved railways in 1971—the driver of each train is given a train staff for each single line section as a token of authority for his train to enter and be in it. A train staff is usually a short wooden staff or metal rod with names of stations at each end of its section marked on it.

With this system at its simplest there is only one staff for each section, so trains must pass through a section alternately in each direction. Where trains need to follow one another, 'train staff and ticket' working may be used; the tickets are either printed card tickets, filled in for each train for which one is issued, or detachable pieces of the train staff for a section. In either case, when given to a driver a ticket authorizes his train to enter a section, provided he is first shown the staff to confirm it is not being carried by a train coming towards him. When the train carrying the ticket arrives at the far end of the section, another may follow, carrying either the train staff or another ticket. Where even greater flexibility is needed, some form of electric train staff system is used. In instruments at each end of a section are stored several train staffs for it. The instruments are connected electrically— once a staff has been removed from either of them, no more can be extracted until it has been replaced, at either end of the section.

Signals control trains. Most familiar are semaphore signals: home signals, with red square-ended arms which instruct drivers to stop their trains when they are 'on', or horizontal, and to proceed when they are 'off', or inclined up or down; and distant signals with yellow fish-tailed arms which repeat the indication of the next home signal to give drivers room to stop if necessary. 'Colour lights' are also used as signals, and so, at the opposite extreme of simplicity, are red and green flags.

What does everyone do who works on a steam railway? Most tasks have more to them than meets the eye. The engine driver, it is clear, not only drives his engine but is responsible for seeing he has authority to proceed. He must also keep to the time-table. In this he is helped or hindered by his companion on the foot-plate, the fireman. He, by feeding the fire with fuel and the boiler with water, endeavours to make them produce the right amount of steam at the right time, depending on whether the train is stationary or moving, heavy or light, going uphill or down. The fireman may also couple and uncouple vehicles, work the points which divert trains from one track to another, or operate electric train staff instruments. At busy stations and yards these jobs are done by shunters and signalmen, the latter also working the signals.

The guard is responsible for the train. Before it leaves he sees, among other things, that the coaches are all coupled together and to engine or tender, that the vacuum brake is working and the handbrake off, that all doors are shut and the station clock shows departure time. Only then does he blow his whistle and wave a green flag to give the driver the 'right away'. He may also issue tickets and check or collect them, or this may be done by booking-clerks and ticket collectors. Somewhere behind the scenes is a controller to ensure that all goes according to plan, and to try to put things right if they do not. Then there are refreshments, souvenirs and books to be sold, and also ordered. In the background are people who maintain locomotives, coaches, wagons, track, bridges, cuttings, embankments, buildings, signals, telephones and all the other things that make up a railway. And there is a management, to arrange time-tables, roster staff, collect members' subscriptions, publicize the railway and plan ahead.

Appendix C
Code of Practice—Association of Railway Preservation Societies

'Applicants for membership of the Association of Railway Preservation Societies must first give an assurance that they conform to and will observe the Code of Practice as set out below. In the event of the applicant being unable to satisfy the Association that it can comply with paragraphs 3 to 13 of the Code of Practice, the Association may at its discretion, if it considers that the failure to comply is in respect of a minor matter only and in the circumstances is reasonable, elect the applicant as an "Associate" Member.

1. The body has satisfied the Association that the objects for which it was formed are attainable, and are likely to prove of benefit to British Railway Preservation, and do not duplicate those of an already established preservation body.

2. The Chairman, Secretary and Treasurer of the body, in addition to a majority of the Committee of Management, are adult persons.

3. In the case of a body whose members are required as a condition of Membership to make an annual subscription, there is a written Constitution, an up-to-date copy of which is lodged with the Association, which includes the following principles:

   (a) The objects for which the body is formed.
   (b) That any member may propose any other member (subject to '2' above) as a candidate for election to the Committee of Management and such election shall be by ballot of members. No member of the Committee of Management may serve for more than 3 years without standing for re-election.
   (c) That proper books of account shall be kept and that at

regular intervals there will be laid before the members a statement of Income and Expenditure and a current Balance Sheet.

(d) That the books of account will be regularly examined by either a Chartered or Certified Accountant or by two members of the body, appointed at a General Meeting, who are not Officers or members of the Committee of Management.

(e) That a general meeting of members will be held at least once every calendar year for the election of officers and the approval of financial accounts.

(f) That in the event of dissolution or winding up of the body, provision has been made for the disposal of the assets of the body.

4. In the case of a body seeking donations from members of the public (not being a body requiring an annual subscription) it has:

(a) Stated the objects for which the body is formed and lodged a copy thereof with the Secretary of the Association together with the names and addresses of the promoters.

(b) Made arrangements
   (i) to keep proper books of account.
  (ii) to prepare a statement of account at the conclusion of the fund or at annual intervals until that time is reached.
 (iii) for each statement to be examined either by a Chartered or Certified Accountant or by two persons approved by the Association.
 (iv) for a copy of the accounts to be lodged with the Secretary of the Association.

(c) Made arrangements for any person who has made a donation to the body to receive a copy of the Statement of Account upon payment of 5 new pence.

5. In the case of a body seeking donations from members of the public towards the purchase of a specific object and which does not raise sufficient money to purchase the object:

(a) The body will return all donations in full to the person who made the donation unless:
  (i) an alternative course of action was indicated at the time the donation was made.
  (ii) there is no record available of the source of the donation.

(b) If there are any monies remaining after the return of donations in the manner aforesaid, such monies unless otherwise determined will be paid direct to the Treasurer for the time being of any Railway Preservation body, being a member of the Association and considered by the promoters of the unsuccessful body to be the most suitable alternative.

6. In the case of a body having obtained donations from members of the public for the purchase of a specific object (not being a body requiring an annual subscription) and which is successful in attaining its object, the body has:

(a) A place where the object can be stored and as soon as practicable placed on public display.

(b) Made reasonable arrangements for the continued preservation of the object without recourse to further appeals for money, except to replace major mechanical items in previously operational locomotives or rolling stock which would be operational but for the defective item.

(c) Made provision for any monies earned from the hiring, leasing or use of the object in any way whatsoever, being used exclusively for the maintenance of the object.

(d) In the event of the dissolution or winding up of the body, made provision for the continued preservation of the object, should it still exist, and made arrangements for the disposal of any surplus assets and taken all reasonable steps to relieve the trustees and/or donors from further liability.

7. When members of the public are to be admitted to the premises of a body, whether on payment of an entrance fee or not, an Insurance Policy will be taken out with a reputable

company to indemnify the body against any claim made against it or a member, by a member of the public for any loss, damage, injury or death whether caused by accident, or negligence or otherwise of the body or a member of the body.

8. When any person is working on behalf of the body they will be covered by an Insurance Policy taken out with a reputable company against any loss, damage, injury or death arising out of this work for which the body or any of its members may be legally liable. Provided that if the person is 21 years of age or over no such cover shall be necessary if he has signed a form of indemnity releasing the body and/or its members or any other person working on behalf of the body from such liability.

9. In the case of a body operating a line the body will limit the financial liability of its members.

10. Any member body shall comply with Sections 32 and 33 (Boilers) and Section 36 (Air Receivers) and Section 27 (Cranes and Lifting Machinery) of the Factories Acts as if that member body and its premises were the occupier of and a factory within the meaning of those Acts and in the case of Boilers and Air Receivers there shall be taken out with a reputable company adequate insurance cover against explosion.

11. In the case of a body operating a line or locomotive(s) the body will obtain adequate Public Liability Cover with a reputable company.

12. Any claim, by a member of the Association, in any public statement or advertisement will be capable of documentary substantiation.

13. In the event of two or more bodies seeking to preserve the same object, or having conflicting aims, they will agree to abide by the decision of 3 arbitrators appointed by the Association.

A.R.P.S. 1st August 1968   Amended, June, 1970'

Useful addresses

To compile a list of addresses, from which further information about preserved railways can be obtained, is as desirable as it is difficult. The difficulty is that the preservation societies and similar bodies described in this book are generally administered from the private addresses of their honorary officials—and so are some of the railways. Officials and addresses alter too frequently for a list here to be reliable—they are best sought in the pages of the railway press. The following railways can, however, be contacted at the addresses shown, and since these are mostly their principal stations it is to be hoped they will prove permanent! Probably the relevant supporting societies could be contacted via the same addresses.

Talyllyn Railway Co.,
Wharf Station,
TOWYN,
Merioneth.

Festiniog Railway Co.,
Harbour Station,
PORTHMADOG,
Caernarvonshire, LL49 9NF

Welshpool and Llanfair Light Railway
Preservation Co. Ltd.,
Llanfair Station,
Llanfair Caereinion,
WELSHPOOL,
Montgomeryshire.

The Bluebell Railway Ltd.,
Sheffield Park Station,
UCKFIELD,
Sussex.

Keighley and Worth Valley Light Railway Ltd.,
Haworth Station,
Haworth,
KEIGHLEY,
Yorkshire,
BD22 8NJ.

The Ravenglass and Eskdale Railway Co. Ltd.,
RAVENGLASS,
Cumberland.

Isle of Man Railway Co.,
PO Box No. 30,
DOUGLAS,
Isle of Man.

Severn Valley Railway Co. Ltd.,
Bridgnorth Railway Station,
BRIDGNORTH,
Shropshire.

Dart Valley Railway,
Buckfastleigh Station,
BUCKFASTLEIGH,
Devon,
TQ11 ODZ.

Lochty Private Railway,
Balbuthie,
KILCONQUHAR,
Fife.

Bibliography

Periodicals

The following magazines, produced by organizations connected with the railways described, have been of much value during preparation of this book:

Talyllyn News	Talyllyn Railway Preservation Society
Festiniog Railway Magazine	Festiniog Railway Society
London Area Group News	Festiniog Railway Society
Llanfair Railway Journal	Welshpool and Llanfair Light Railway Preservation Co. Ltd.
*Bluebell News**	Bluebell Railway Preservation Society
*The Old Run**	Middleton Railway Trust
*Push and Pull**	Keighley and Worth Valley Railway Preservation Society
R. & E.R. Newsletter	Ravenglass and Eskdale Railway Preservation Society Ltd.
*Steam Railway News**	Isle of Man Steam Railway Supporters' Association
*Severn Valley Railway News**	Severn Valley Railway Co. Ltd.
*Bulliver**	Dart Valley Railway Association
Sittingbourne and Kemsley Light Railway Newsletter	Locomotive Club of Great Britain
*Chaloner**	Leighton Buzzard Narrow Gauge Railway Society
*Foxfield News**	Foxfield Light Railway Society

These magazines are issued to members of the organizations concerned; those marked * are also sold to the general public.

I have consulted various issues of the following periodicals:
Railway Magazine
Railway World
Steam Alive!
Railway Forum (Steam)
Narrow Gauge Telegraph
Standard Gauge Standard

The two last-named are newspaper format annual publications published respectively by Welsh narrow-gauge lines and certain standard-gauge lines.

Books and Pamphlets
Those I have consulted are:

Talyllyn Railway:
L. T. C. Rolt, *Railway Adventure*, Constable, 1953
L. T. C. Rolt (Editor), *Talyllyn Century*, David & Charles, Dawlish 1965
TRPS (Editor), *Talyllyn Handbook*, David & Charles, Newton Abbot, 1968

Festiniog Railway:
J. I. C. Boyd, *The Festiniog Railway*, Oakwood Press, Lingfield, 1956 (vol. I), 1959 (vol. II)
M. J. T. Lewis, *How Ffestiniog Got Its Railway*, The Railway and Canal Historical Society, Caterham, 1965
C. E. Lee, *Narrow Gauge Railways in North Wales*, The Railway Publishing Co. Ltd., 1945
Festiniog Railway Guide Book, Festiniog Rly., Co., Portmadoc, 1971

Welshpool and Llanfair Light Railway:
Welshpool and Llanfair Light Railway Illustrated Guide, Welshpool and Llanfair Light Railway Preservation Co. Ltd., Llanfair Caereinion, 1969
The Llanfair Railway Companion, W & LLRP Co. Ltd., Llanfair Caereinion, 1969
J. I. C. Boyd, *Narrow Gauge Railways in Mid-Wales*, Oakwood Press, Lingfield, 1965 (also for Talyllyn Railway)

Bluebell Railway:
T. C. Cole, *Steaming On!*, Bluebell Railway Preservation Society, Sheffield Park, 1971

Middleton Railway:
The Middleton Colliery Railway, Leeds, Middleton Railway Trust, Leeds, 1970

Worth Valley Railway:
J. A. Cox, *Worth Valley Railway Guide,* Keighley and Worth Valley Railway Preservation Society, Haworth, 1969
J. A. Cox, *Keighley and Worth Valley Railway Stockbook,* K & WVRPS, Haworth, 1970
R. O. T. Povey, *The History of the Keighley and Worth Valley Railway,* K & WVRPS, Haworth, 1970

Ravenglass and Eskdale Railway:
The Ravenglass and Eskdale Railway Handbook, Ravenglass and Eskdale Railway Co. Ltd., Ravenglass, 1970
Ratty Year, R & ER Co. Ltd., Ravenglass, 1971
W. J. K. Davies, *The Ravenglass and Eskdale Railway,* David and Charles, Newton Abbot, 1968

Isle of Man Railway:
I. Macnab, *A History and Description of The Isle of Man Railway,* Greenlake Publications, 1945
J. I. C. Boyd, *The Isle of Man Railway,* Oakwood Press, Lingfield, 1962
Railways in the Isle of Man, Isle of Man Tourist Board, Douglas, 1971

Severn Valley Railway:
D. N. Cooke and D. C. Williams, *Severn Valley Railway Guide,* Severn Valley Railway Co. Ltd., Bridgnorth, 1971
D. C. Williams, *Severn Valley Railway Stock Book,* SVR Co. Ltd., Bridgnorth, 1971
Sir G. Nabarro MP, *Severn Valley Steam,* Routledge and Kegan Paul, 1971
D. J. Smith, *The Severn Valley Railway,* Town and Country Press Ltd., Bracknell, 1970

Dart Valley Railway:
The Dart Valley Railway, Ian Allan Ltd., 1969
C. G. Woodford, *Stock Book of the Dart Valley Railway,* Dart Valley Railway Association, Buckfastleigh, 1971

Sittingbourne and Kemsley Light Railway:
A. G. Wells, *Bowater's Sittingbourne Railway*, Locomotive Club of Great Britain, Rochester, 1971
Leighton Buzzard Narrow Gauge Railway:
S. A. Leleux, *The Leighton Buzzard Light Railway*, Oakwood Press, Lingfield, 1969.

General background

L. T. C. Rolt, *Red for Danger*, Pan Books Ltd., 1971
W. J. K. Davies, *Light Railways—their rise and decline*, Ian Allan Ltd., 1964 (appendix G quotes the Light Railways Act, 1896)
Railway Construction and Operation Requirements for Passenger Lines and Recommendations for Goods Lines of the Minister of Transport, H.M. Stationery Office, 1966

The dates above are those of the editions consulted—in many instances earlier and/or later editions have been published, sometimes by other publishers.

Acknowledgments

I am most grateful to the many people who have helped, and particularly indebted to the following:

Talyllyn Railway: J. L. H. Bate, R. A. Hope, L. T. C. Rolt, D. W. Woodhouse.

Festiniog Railway: P. Dukes, A. G. W. Garraway, A. Heywood, N. A. Pearce, M. Schumann.

Welshpool and Llanfair Light Railway: M. Polglaze, A. E. Thorndike.

Bluebell Railway: M. J. Mason, H. May.

Middleton Railway: J. Bushell, J. Edwards.

Worth Valley Railway: J. A. Cox, R. S. Greenwood, I. Johnson.

Ravenglass and Eskdale Railway: D. Ferreira, K. Haynes, The Lord Wakefield of Kendal.

Isle of Man Railway: A. Beard, A. M. B. Crookall, W. Lambden.

Severn Valley Railway: J. C. George, H. C. C. Mossop.

Dart Valley Railway: J. B. Cogar, J. T. Holder, R. D. N. Salisbury.

Sittingbourne and Kemsley Light Railway: M. Burton.

Leighton Buzzard Narrow Gauge Railway: M. A. Lilley.

Foxfield Light Railway: T. D. A. Civil.

Lochty Private Railway: J. B. Cameron.

North Yorkshire Moors Railway: A. K. Peterson.

Romney, Hythe and Dymchurch Railway: J. B. Hollingsworth.

Chasewater Light Railway: D. A. Ives.

North Norfolk Railway: J. B. Snell.

Yorkshire Dales Railway Co. Ltd.: E. Black.

Lakeside and Haverthwaite Railway: J. Houghton.

General: P. R. Davis (Transport Trust); T. Mervyn Jones (Wales Tourist Board); Captain P. Manisty, RN (Ret'd) (Association of Railway Preservation Societies); A. G. W. Garraway (Association of Minor Railways, and Narrow Gauge Railways of Wales Joint Marketing Panel); J. Wintle (B.R.B.).

Maps Nos. 2, 3, 4, 5 and 6 are based upon the Ordnance Survey Map with the sanction of the Controller of H.M. Stationery Office, Crown copyright reserved.

The letter to the Editor of *The Times*, on page 26, is reproduced by kind permission of its writer, L. T. C. Rolt; the extract from *The Trains We Loved* on page 45 is reproduced by kind permission of its author, C. Hamilton Ellis, and publishers, George Allen & Unwin Ltd. and Pan Books Ltd.; and the Code of Practice of the A.R.P.S. is reproduced by kind permission of the chairman, Captain P. Manisty RN (Ret'd).

R. S. Greenwood, as legal adviser to the A.R.P.S., was most helpful over the section of chapter one which describes companies, etc., of various kinds. My wife Elisabeth has somehow managed, very kindly, to type most of the manuscript despite counter-demands on her attention from a small and very mischievous puppy.

Index